RAF
COASTAL COMMAND
A PICTORIAL HISTORY
KEITH WILSON

AMBERLEY

First published 2020

Amberley Publishing
The Hill, Stroud
Gloucestershire, GL5 4EP

www.amberley-books.com

Copyright © Keith Wilson, 2020

The right of Keith Wilson to be identified as
the Author of this work has been asserted in
accordance with the Copyrights, Designs and
Patents Act 1988.

ISBN: 978 1 4456 9768 0 (print)
ISBN: 978 1 4456 9769 7 (ebook)

British Library Cataloguing in Publication Data.
A catalogue record for this book is available from
the British Library.

Typeset in 10pt on 12.5pt Celeste.
Typesetting by Aura Technology and Software
Services, India. Printed in UK.

Contents

Introduction

Constant Endeavour

When the Royal Flying Corps (RFC) and the Royal Naval Air Service (RNAS) were formally amalgamated on 1 April 1918 to form the Royal Air Force, it began a conflict with the Admiralty which would rage for many years. At the time of the formation, the Admiralty had reluctantly handed over 2,949 aircraft (including seaplanes and flying boats) as well as transferring 5,378 officers and 49,688 men. The men were given an opportunity of returning to the Royal Navy, assuming they did so within the first three months, but few did. However, the Admiralty's determination to regain control of any RAF unit involved in so-called 'naval areas of interest' remained. It was a situation which would undermine the maritime units of the RAF for the next two decades and led to many unsatisfactory compromises being made.

Coastal Area came into being in 1919, under RAF control. Its role was little more than 'fleet co-operation' and consisted of a single reconnaissance/spotting squadron, along with a 'fighting' Flight at RAF Leuchars, half a torpedo squadron at Gosport, No. 230 (Flying Boat) Squadron at Felixstowe and the Naval Co-operation Flight of seaplanes at Calshot.

The severe neglect of maritime aviation continued almost all the way through the inter-war period, primarily due to continued disagreements between the Royal Navy and the RAF over the ownership, leadership, roles and investment in maritime air power. Even in 1937, the Admiralty's main concern was the return of the Fleet Air Arm to the Royal Navy. The financial state of the British economy, particularly following the First World War, had not helped, with very limited funds being available for any kind of spending on the Armed Forces.

It was against this background that when Coastal Command was created on 14 July 1936, it was under-equipped, understaffed and under-prepared for what was heading its way. Despite some re-equipment in the three years leading up to the start of the Second World War, it was no surprise when A.V. Alexander, the First Lord of the Admiralty, referred to it as the 'Cinderella Service' in November 1940!

However, the importance of its role during the Second World War, particularly defending the supply lines during the Battle of the Atlantic along with the protection of Allied convoys against the menace of the German and Italian U-boats, cannot be understated. In fact, it was absolutely crucial. Then there was the Air-Sea Rescue capability, the Meteorological Research and Photographic Reconnaissance, all of which made significant contributions to the war effort.

Coastal Command saw action from the very first day of the Second World War right up until the very last day. It completed more than a million flying hours, over 240,000 operations, and was credited with the destruction of 212 U-boats and 366 German transport vessels, while damaging a further 134. It rescued a total of 10,334 people including 5,721 Allied crew members, 277 enemy personnel and 4,665 non-aircrew. However, it paid a very high cost for its efforts, losing 2,060 aircraft with 5,866 Coastal Command personnel killed in action. The bravery and gallantry demonstrated by Coastal Command led to the award of four Victoria Crosses (of whom only one survived the war), seventeen George Medals and eighty-two Distinguished Service Orders alone.

The end of the Second World War saw a rapid rundown in the strength of Coastal Command, with the immediate disbandment of its combat units and the transfer of many aircraft to Transport Command. The end of the war also signalled the end of the Lend-Lease arrangements with the US Government in August 1945, meaning large numbers of critical aircraft, such as the very long-range (VLR) B-17 Fortress and B-24 Liberator, were returned to the USA, thereby creating further reductions in the Command's strength and capabilities. With money in short supply, there was little chance of any re-equipment and the Command had to wait until the Avro Shackleton MR.1 began to enter service in 1951 before any new capability became available.

Despite its downsizing and reductions in capabilities, Coastal Command was still required to assist in various theatres. Its Sunderland aircraft assisted in the Berlin Airlift in 1948, while in 1956 it assisted with the movement of troops into Cyprus as well as anti-smuggling patrols. Later that year Coastal Command Shackleton aircraft once again assisted with an airlift, this time into the Suez region. It was also involved with conflicts in Malaya, Oman, Jordan, Kuwait, Borneo, British Guiana, South Arabia and the 'Beira Patrols' in and around Rhodesia, acquitting themselves well in all operations during subsequent years.

The Cold War brought a change in the perceived threat – this time from the Soviet Union, with Coastal Command being on the sharp end of the threat from the Soviet Navy and, in particular, its submarine force. This became heightened in 1962 with the Cuban Missile Crisis, when Coastal Command were placed on high alert monitoring the movement of Soviet ships carrying aircraft, missiles and other equipment across the Atlantic to Cuba. Thankfully, a peaceful resolution to the problem was eventually found.

In 1969, the special-purpose maritime reconnaissance Nimrod MR.1 was due to enter service with Coastal Command, which it did on 2 October. Less than eight weeks later, on 27 November 1969, Coastal Command was disbanded when it was absorbed into the new Strike Command.

The part played by Coastal Command during the Second World War has long been overshadowed by the more glamorous exploits of Fighter Command and by the rather controversial campaign waged by Bomber Command. Coastal Command is now best remembered for its significant role in the Battle of the Atlantic, the campaign upon which Britain's very survival depended, as did all further campaigns during the Second World War. All of Coastal Command's success was achieved despite being starved of equipment and resources for much of the time. Coastal Command can be rightly proud of its contributions and achievements during the Second World War.

This book is not an attempt to create the definitive history of Coastal Command – that is just not possible within the pages available! There are more detailed volumes in existence, with much greater detail for the reader, if required. However, this book should provide a potted history in pictorial form of what was a key RAF Command, particularly during the Second World War.

Images

As the title suggests, this is predominately a picture-led volume. In selecting the images for this book, I have often been obliged to choose between quality and originality. I have gone to considerable lengths to include as many previously unpublished images as possible but there are only a finite number of images held within the corridors of the excellent Air Historical Branch library. One must also bear in mind that while many of these images were taken by members of the RAF Photographic Unit or shot unofficially by other service personnel, many were taken in action against the enemy, with F24 cameras either in a fixed position or hand-held by a crew member, such as the wireless operator. Others were taken by G45 gun cameras facing forward and operated when the pilot pressed the firing mechanism.

Where a poor-quality image has been used, it is because I decided the interest value of the subject matter has warranted the decision, making it a better choice than perhaps a familiar, previously published image.

I have thoroughly enjoyed researching this volume, the fifth in the 'A Pictorial History' series for Amberley Publishing. I sincerely hope this pictorial history of RAF Coastal Command enlightens and, more importantly, entertains the reader.

Keith Wilson
Ramsey, Cambridgeshire
October 2020

Acknowledgements

A project of this nature requires the help and support of many people, who have contributed in different ways to make the book possible. The author would like to offer his sincere thanks to the following:

Sebastian Cox at the Air Historical Branch, RAF Northolt, for providing the Branch's support with access to the collection of images and information, along with his encouragement and sense of humour.

My thanks must also go to Lee Barton at the Air Historical Branch for his unwavering enthusiasm, vision and attention to detail during the image selection process. Also, thanks must go to his research skills, unearthing new information and responding to the never-ending stream of questions.

Thanks are also due to John Swain for the donation of books from the late Harold Swain selection, which provided an excellent source of research material.

At Amberley Publishing I would like to thank Kevin Paul, Louis Archard, Fraser Searle, Connor Stait and Aaron Phull for their considerable input at key stages during the book's production.

Sincere thanks are due to my sons Sam and Oliver. Thank you for your patience and support throughout the project; I couldn't have done it without you.

Finally, my special thanks must go to Carol – for being there to support me throughout the project.

The Formation of Coastal Command (1936–39)

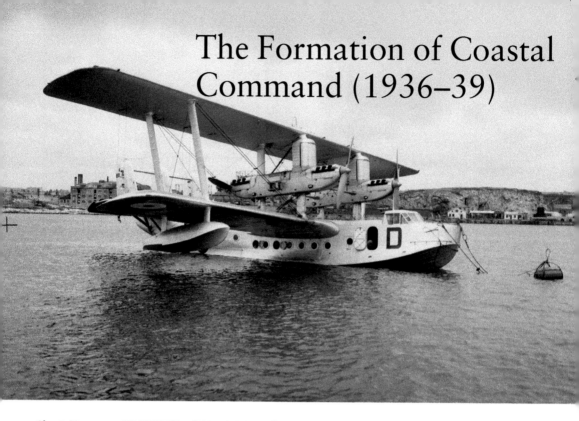

Short Singapore III K8856/D of No. 210 Squadron moored at Mount Batten, Plymouth, in May 1937. This aircraft was one of the last of the stately Singapore aircraft to be built and was initially delivered to No. 228 Squadron. (*Crown Copyright/Air Historical Branch image H-273*)

During the mid-1930s, the British Government had become increasingly concerned after hearing reports of a major German rearmament programme. In July 1934, following a powerful speech in the House of Commons by Winston Churchill, the mood in the country began to change and for the first time in many years, an increase in defence expenditure seemingly became acceptable to the majority. Shortly afterwards, a series of RAF 'Expansion Schemes' were announced; Scheme 'C', aimed at proposing to double the strength of the Metropolitan Air Force, received approval in May 1935. However, it soon became clear that it wasn't just flying assets that the RAF desperately required, as its overall organisation – especially of the home-based units – was considered somewhat lacking.

On 13 July 1936, Air Defence Great Britain and the Areas were abolished and on the following day RAF Commands were formed – based upon function rather than location, which had been the previous organisational preference. The RAF was then restructured into Fighter, Bomber and Coastal Commands.

The old Coastal Area had effectively become Coastal Command and with the change of name it moved its headquarters to Lee-on-Solent, with the command renaming being handled by Air Marshal Sir Arthur Longmore, before handing over command to Air Marshal Philip Joubert de la Ferté on 24 August 1936.

From the outset Coastal Command was primarily seen as a provider of general reconnaissance; and even then, it was significantly under-equipped to fulfil that role effectively. Maritime air units never made up more than 12 per cent of British air strength. Its pre-expansion strength was just five squadrons, of which four were flying boats, and probably most of those were obsolete.

With the expansion scheme in place, Coastal Command progressively increased its strength to eighteen maritime squadrons by 18 September 1938, with a total strength of just 176 aircraft. Some sixteen of these squadrons were allotted to trade defence, but given Trenchard's policy of developing bombers for the maritime arm which could bolster the air offensive, it meant that no specialist anti-submarine warfare (ASW) aircraft were developed as the Air Ministry was clearly uninterested in any aircraft which could not provide the bomber function. This was a decision that would eventually come to haunt the RAF once the Second World War had commenced.

Air Marshal Philip Joubert de la Ferté, the Command's AOC, was highly critical of the Air Ministry's attitude towards his service, as he felt it was not being taken seriously. In 1937, several exercises were conducted by Coastal Command in co-operation with Royal Navy submarines of the Home Fleet in order to judge the surface fleet's defensive capability against submarine and air attack. Despite a number of lessons learned from the First World War, little or no attention was paid to the problem of attacking submarines from the air, particularly in connection with convoy patrols and protection. It seemed that owing to a misplaced faith in the imperfect ASDIC invention (an underwater anti-submarine detection system which was similar to the US Navy's SONAR, meaning Sound Navigation Ranging), the Royal Navy no longer considered U-boats a threat to the British sea lanes. How wrong they were to be proven!

There was to be one saving grace for both services and that was the construction of a Combined Headquarters, which would enable a rapid collaboration in maritime operations – something that subsequently proved particularly helpful.

However, it was not all negative. The first fruits of the expansion scheme saw the arrival of the Avro Anson – Coastal Command's first reconnaissance landplane since the First World War – into service. The first aircraft, due to be delivered to No. 48 Squadron, were diverted to the School of Air Navigation at RAF Manston to provide suitable air training for the large number of aircrew that would be required going forward. Shortly afterwards, No. 236 Squadron equipped with the new Anson and they began training the multi-engine pilots required for both Bomber and Coastal Command. Three more squadrons had been formed by 1937.

With the arrival of a new AOC on 16 August 1937 – Air Marshal Sir Frederick Bowhill – a major reorganisation was undertaken, which included doubling the size of the number of squadrons at Pembroke Dock, where they received a mixture of Scapa, London and Singapore flying boats. That said, these were hardly state-of-the-art aircraft and highlighted Coastal Command's limited equipment. There were still outstanding orders for the last of the classic biplanes – the Supermarine Stranraer – which did not reach an operational Coastal Command squadron until June 1938.

There were, however, deliveries of the Bristol Beaufort and Blackburn Botha, along with the Saunders-Roe (Saro) Lerwick (flying boat) ordered in 1936. The first two types were due to replace the Anson and Vildebeest aircraft in the general reconnaissance/torpedo bomber roles. History will show that the Beaufort was to suffer significant teething problems before finally entering service with No. 22 Squadron at RAF Thorney Island in November 1939.

The Blackburn B.26 Botha was another story, however, and was just about to enter service when the Second World War broke out. It had been ordered 'straight off the drawing board', with contracts placed for 442 aircraft initially, later increased to 580. Initial deliveries were made to No. 608 (North Riding) Squadron of the Royal Auxiliary Service, where they replaced Anson aircraft. The Botha continued in service with No. 608 Squadron, chiefly on North Sea patrols, until 6 November 1940, when they were withdrawn from operational service after just 308 sorties. The Botha was seriously underpowered and lacked directional control on one engine, such that numerous fatal accidents followed. Its shortcomings were such that the type was not issued to other squadrons as had been planned, but was instead employed in operational training duties.

By the end of 1937, the Air Ministry finally notified Coastal Command of its strategic tasks and provided estimates of the number of aircraft required to fulfil them:

1. Protection of trade (213 aircraft);
2. Reconnaissance in support of Fleet operations (84 aircraft);
3. Co-operation with the Royal Navy (42 aircraft).

This decision still left several questions unanswered and continued to cause consternation within the corridors of Coastal Command HQ.

In May 1939, the first of the new Lockheed Hudson aircraft were delivered to No. 224 Squadron at RAF Leuchars and were able to fill the general reconnaissance gap left by the delay of the Beaufort and Botha. In June 1939, a contract was placed with Lockheed for a further 200 Hudson aircraft (along with 200 Harvard training aircraft for the RAF) – causing a storm of protest from British aircraft manufacturers. Fortunately, the protests were ignored and an additional commitment was made to accept up to 250 Hudson aircraft if they could be delivered before the end of 1939. The figure was actually achieved by the end of October of that year, however, by then all restrictions had been lifted.

The Royal Navy were still convinced of their ASDIC capabilities against the German U-boat fleet so any further re-equipping of Coastal Command in this role against the German U-boat fleet was considered unnecessary. In addition, the only ordnance available for use by Coastal Command were standard 100 and 250lb General Purpose bombs for use against surface vessels, with 'special' 100lb ordnance for attacks against submarine targets; the latter was still in production although it had been proved to be utterly useless as early as 1917. This problem was compounded by the lack of a suitable low-level bomb sight, the force relying on the human 'eyeball' to hit the target.

The situation with torpedoes was a little better, although nothing had been done in connection with the significantly faster dropping speeds of more modern aircraft; the same applied to aerial mines. Development of the magnetic 'A' Mk1 torpedo had started ahead of the war but it was not ready for production until early 1940.

By April 1939, with Hitler on the rampage, international tensions had started to rise. They reached fever pitch in the summer when an attack on Poland was clearly imminent and preliminary mobilisation commenced on 24 July, with units moving to a war footing in the following month.

Meanwhile, Hitler had given instructions for his U-boat fleet to start leaving port and fourteen departed for the Atlantic on 19 August, with the battle cruisers (nicknamed 'pocket battleships' by the British) *Admiral Graf Spee* and *Deutschland* leaving a few days later. Organised patrols by Coastal Command were not started until 24 August, so none of these movements were detected. A further sixteen U-boats left port on 25 August under cover of dense fog, so these were also missed. It was a poor start for the British forces.

At the start of the Second World War on 3 September 1939, Coastal Command was equipped with the following aircraft:

Avro Anson	8 squadrons composed of 24 aircraft each
Avro Anson/Lockheed Hudson	1 squadron composed of 24 aircraft
Short Sunderland	3 squadrons composed of 6 aircraft each

Vickers Vildebeest	2 squadrons composed of 15 aircraft each
Saro London	2 squadrons composed of 6 aircraft each
Supermarine Stranraer	1 squadron composed of 6 aircraft

In addition, there were the following training establishments:

The Torpedo Training School;
The School of General Reconnaissance;
The Seaplane Training Squadron.

The actual aircraft strength of the Command (including training establishments) was:

Avro Anson	301
Lockheed Hudson	53
Saro London	17
Short Sunderland	27
Supermarine Stranraer	9
Vickers Vildebeest	30

In addition to the above, the Command had several one-off communications aircraft, which in all provided a total force of almost 450 aircraft, of which perhaps half were truly front-line equipment – although not all of them would have been serviceable or operational.

A Saunders-Roe (Saro) Cloud, serial number K2898, of 'B' Flight of the Seaplane Training Squadron at Calshot, photographed in 1934 while passing the Calshot Spit. Students would conduct their initial seaplane training with 'A' Flight on the Sea Tutor before continuing with 'B' Flight on the Cloud, and then completing their training with 'C' Flight, usually on the Southampton. (*Crown Copyright/Air Historical Branch image H-251*)

The prototype Supermarine Southampton MkIV, S1648, which was later renamed 'Scapa' in October 1933. It was photographed in June 1934 while undergoing trials with No. 202 Squadron on Malta. (*Crown Copyright/Air Historical Branch image H-839*)

Supermarine Scapa serial number K4191 was powered by a pair of Kestrel III engines. (*Crown Copyright/Air Historical Branch image H-1840*)

Short Singapore serial number K4577 was photographed at Felixstowe while undergoing armament and equipment trials in 1935. It was later transferred to No. 209 Squadron in September 1935 and No. 203 Squadron in October 1935 before being struck off charge on 3 January 1940. (*Crown Copyright/Air Historical Branch image H-1841*)

A Fairey IIIF twin-float seaplane, serial number S1454, of the Seaplane Training Squadron was photographed while preparing to launch from a slipway at Calshot. The Seaplane Training Squadron formed part of Coastal Area and came into being on 1 October 1931 when the RAS Seaplane Training Flight was renamed. It was later absorbed into Coastal Command upon their creation in July 1936. S1454 was the first of ten Fairey IIIF (DC) – dual control – aircraft constructed. (*Crown Copyright/Air Historical Branch image H-146*)

Three Supermarine Southampton flying boats – serial numbers N9900/3, N9901/4 (both Mk I aircraft) and S1232/2 (a Mk II aircraft) – of No. 201 Squadron based at Calshot. No. 201 Squadron received their Southampton flying boats in January 1929 and continued to operate them until December 1936, when they were eventually replaced with Saro London flying boats. (*Crown Copyright/Air Historical Branch image AHB-GSR-10038*)

A Charles E. Brown image of Supermarine I K8345 being hoisted aboard HMS *Devonshire*. Delivered to Mount Batten on 25 September 1936, the aircraft was transferred to No. 711 Flight two months later for service with HMS *Devonshire*. (*Crown Copyright/Air Historical Branch image CEB-5655-4*)

Vickers Vildebeest II K2937/15 of No. 100 Squadron dropping a torpedo during a practice sortie in the Far East during 1936. (*Crown Copyright/Air Historical Branch image H-357*)

Short Rangoon flying boat S1433 of No. 203 Squadron was photographed in flight in 1935. A total of six Rangoon flying boats were built for the RAF and were initially used by No. 203 Squadron before being transferred to No. 210 Squadron, where they remained until September 1936, only having the very briefest career within Coastal Command. (*Crown Copyright/Air Historical Branch image H-781*)

Saro London II K5911 of No. 204 Squadron at Mount Batten, near Plymouth, photographed in April 1937. (*Crown Copyright/Air Historical Branch image H-254*)

A Vickers Vildebeest III, serial number K4163, of B Flight at Gosport during a sortie on 21 May 1937. (*Crown Copyright/Air Historical Branch image H-355*)

A Short Singapore III flying boat, K6921/Z of No. 209 Squadron was photographed while preparing to leave its Mount Batten home, near Plymouth, for an anti-piracy patrol during the Spanish Civil War on 18 September 1937. (*Crown Copyright/Air Historical Branch image H-276*)

Ground crew of No. 204 Squadron preparing to refuel Saro London II K6929 at Mount Batten on 18 September 1937. (*Crown Copyright/Air Historical Branch image AHB-GSR-7943*)

Saro London II K6929 of No. 204 Squadron undergoing a compass calibration at Mount Batten on 28 November 1937 prior to departing the UK for Australia. K6929 was one of five aircraft which, under the command of Wing Commander K.B. Lloyd, undertook a six-month cruise to Australia to mark the 150th anniversary of the foundation of the University of Sydney. (*Crown Copyright/Air Historical Branch image AHB-GSR-8012*)

Engine fitters servicing the Armstrong-Siddeley Serval radial engines fitted to Saro Cloud K3725 during 1937. *(Crown Copyright/Air Historical Branch image H-252)*

Pigeons are loaded on to a Saro London flying boat at Calshot on 2 September 1938, just ahead of an operational patrol. (*Crown Copyright/Air Historical Branch image AHB-GSR-9344*)

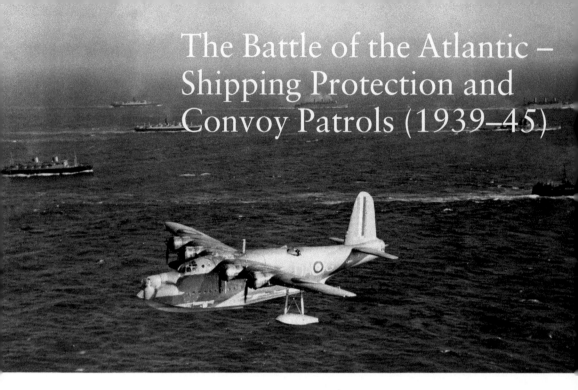

The Battle of the Atlantic – Shipping Protection and Convoy Patrols (1939–45)

Sunderland I L2163/DA-G of No. 210 Squadron, based at Oban, was photographed on shipping escort duties on 31 July 1940. This aircraft was later sunk in a gale at Stranraer on 15 January 1941, but after being recovered was used for training purposes. (*Crown Copyright/Air Historical Branch image CH-832*)

As a small island nation, Britain relied heavily upon importing supplies – food, manufacturing materials, armaments and, later, troops. Most, if not all, of this material arrived in the UK by sea, so the regular merchant navy convoys crossing the Atlantic from both the United States and Canada were crucial to Britain's survival.

At the outbreak of the war, the Royal Navy was still confident about protecting these crucial convoys against the perceived attacks from the German navy's U-boat pack, as well as their fleet of capital ships. Initially, in order to get to the Atlantic hunting grounds, the U-boats had to complete the dangerous transit through the North Sea and around Britain's northern waters, or alternatively through the English Channel, which was guarded by the Royal and French navies. At the time, the French navy was responsible for covering half of the Atlantic shipping routes and provided half of the Allied defensive forces available. Initially, the balance of power slightly favoured the Allies but the events of April to June 1940 significantly altered the balance of both naval and air power as the German forces conquered Denmark, Norway, Holland, Belgium and France. Having now occupied these countries, it enabled the Luftwaffe to operate from French airfields along the coast and the Kriegsmarine to operate from French ports along the Atlantic coast, hundreds of miles closer to the all-important Atlantic shipping lanes.

Scarecrow Patrols

In the early days of the Second World War Coastal Command had limited resources and were often forced to compromise. On the simple assumption that submarines could not complete an attack while submerged below periscope height, the Allies used 'Scarecrow' patrols in the hope of preventing a potential attack, especially around harbours and their inlets. These were flown by a variety of – often unarmed – aircraft, the main purpose being to force the attacker below the water. In December 1939, Coastal Command created six Coastal Patrol Flights (CPFs), located at strategic locations around Britain's coastline, with each CPF being established with up to nine aircraft. The aircraft allocated were de Havilland Tiger Moth aircraft, except for the operation at St Eval (No. 6 CPF), which flew de Havilland Hornet Moth aircraft. The sole armament of these aircraft consisted of a signal pistol, while communication was usually provided by a pair of homing pigeons carried in a wicker basket positioned in the front cockpit. The aircraft would normally operate in pairs, so if a U-boat was identified, one aircraft could return to base to summon assistance. They also created tactics with Royal Navy vessels; by firing a green Very light signal and then circling, they could indicate the location of the submarine.

New Equipment Fails to Perform

During the early part of the Second World War, the Avro Anson was the backbone of the Command. A limited re-equipment had been launched in 1937 but two of the three aircraft that arrived with Coastal Command just ahead of, and during the early part of, the Second World War proved to be abject failures – the Saunders-Roe (Saro) A.36 Lerwick and the Blackburn B.26 Botha (which was described on page 9 in Chapter 1).

The Saro Lerwick flying boat had been intended to supplement the Short Sunderland in service, but its design was flawed and only a small number were completed. They had an appalling service record and a high accident rate; of twenty-one aircraft built, ten were lost in accidents and another for an unknown reason. The first three aircraft were used as prototypes, with the first flight being recorded on 31 October 1938. Immediately, the Lerwick was found to be unstable, both in the air and on water. Aside from structural problems, the Lerwick had a particularly unpleasant characteristic if the aircraft suffered an engine failure as it could not even maintain height while the torque of the other (good) engine on maximum power prevented the aircraft being flown in a straight line. It would invariably fly in slowly descending circles until making contact with the water!

In mid-1938, four Lerwick aircraft were allocated to No. 240 Squadron at Pembroke Dock but by October the squadron had ceased flying them and reverted back to the older and slower Saro London flying boats. Despite not wanting them, a number of Lerwick aircraft were delivered to No. 209 Squadron while detached at Falmouth but the squadron soon began losing aircraft to accidents. During their short service with No. 209 Squadron, all of the Lerwick aircraft were twice grounded for safety modifications. Amazingly, on only two occasions did a Lerwick ever attack a U-boat and neither of the submarines was damaged!

Hudson Enters the Fray

Shortly after the Second World War began, many squadrons that were initially equipped with the faithful Anson were re-equipped with the Lockheed Hudson. The new aircraft were of particular assistance in maintaining patrols in the Norwegian Sea – the route that the German navy would most likely take in order to get into the Atlantic to attack the shipping convoys. On 8 October, the crew of a No. 224 Squadron Hudson sighted a battleship, a cruiser and four destroyers off the south-west coast of Norway. Unfortunately, when Wellington aircraft of Bomber Command were despatched to attack, heavy rain and low cloud prevented the bombers making contact.

However, on the same day, a 'battle flight' of three Hudson aircraft from No. 224 Squadron came upon a Dornier Do18 flying boat, which was attacked, forcing the Dornier to alight on the sea and the crew abandon their aircraft. It was Coastal Command's first victory of the war by aircraft based in the UK.

Magnetic Mines and the DWI

Aside from the U-boat attacks on Allied shipping, the German navy provided another headache in the form of magnetic mines, which were dropped in British coastal waters. An initial and rather risky solution was to recover and defuse the mines; however, this dangerous method did provide the 'boffins' with an eventual antidote, which meant the fitting of a cable around the mine and passing an electric current through it, effectively neutralising its magnetic field.

A somewhat stranger solution came in the form of specially modified Wellington bombers, equipped with a giant ring-shaped electro-magnet. The name given to the modification – DWI (Directional Wireless Installation) – was a deliberately misleading code-name; the apparatus allowed the aircraft to explode mines by flying low over the water. This solution was placed under the administrative control of No. 16 Group, Coastal Command, and the first DWI-equipped Wellington was ready for operations in January 1940.

ASV II Radar

Air-to-surface Vessel Mk II or ASV Mk II for short was an airborne sea-surface search radar developed by the Ministry of Defence prior to the Second World War and was the first aircraft-mounted radar to be used operationally. It was widely used by aircraft of Coastal Command and the Fleet Air Arm.

The system was developed between 1937 and early 1939 and followed the accidental detection of ships in the English Channel by an air-to-air radar then under development. The original ASV Mk I entered service in early 1940 but was soon replaced by the much-improved Mk II. That said, while the Mk II was fine against large capital vessels, it was of limited ability against smaller vessels such as U-boats.

It was a Swordfish equipped with a Mk II radar set that located the *Bismarck* in heavy overcast skies before torpedoing her, which ultimately led to the ship's destruction the following day.

Merchant Ship Fighter Unit (MSFU)

The MSFU was created to provide pilots, crew and support personnel, and aircraft to operate from thirty-five merchant vessels that had been equipped with a catapult on the bow. Known as Catapult Aircraft Movement (CAM) ships, this was a stop-gap initiative to provide air support to convoys out of reach of land-based aircraft in the early part of the Second World War, when aircraft carrier support was rare, or non-existent.

The aircraft operated by the MSFU were converted Mk I Hurricanes, often Battle of Britain veterans that were near the end of their useful lives. The single catapult consisted of an 85-foot rail, along which a launch trolley powered by a battery of 3-inch rockets would propel the Hurricane over a distance of 60 feet. With 30º of flap deployed the aircraft would stagger into the air.

The downside of the system was that the pilot was not able to recover back to the ship. Instead, he would be forced to bailout or ditch the aircraft once the fuel had been exhausted. While every effort was made to recover the pilot, some operational factors – such as the convoy being under attack from U-boats – may have meant that a vessel was not detached to collect the pilot. On the convoys to Russia, the very low sea temperatures meant that the pilot had a very low potential survival rate after landing in the sea, making the launch almost a suicide mission. CAM fighters were credited with seven kills and their presence apparently discouraged the long-range Focke-Wulf FW200 Condor aircraft from pressing home attacks on convoys. CAM ships were replaced by escort carriers in 1943.

New Equipment Arrives Although Losses Rise

Between 1940 and 1941, new equipment was arriving at Coastal Command, in the form of the ASV-equipped Armstrong Whitworth Whitley, Bristol Blenheim IV and Beaufort aircraft, in addition to an increasing number of Short Sunderland and Lockheed Hudson aircraft. The new Catalina flying boat joined Coastal Command in early 1941, along with ASV-equipped Wellington bombers. Despite the new additions, convoy losses had increased – particularly in the Atlantic – and the British war effort was feeling the effects. What the Command really lacked was an aircraft with Very Long Range (VLR) capabilities, to operate convoy support operations much further from home.

VLR Equipment Becomes Available

Boeing B-17 Fortress I aircraft had joined Bomber Command as early as 1941, and when replaced with the newer, more capable Fortress II in 1942, the remaining Fortress I aircraft were handed over to Coastal Command.

The first Consolidated B-24 Liberator aircraft were delivered across the Atlantic in March 1941, although the earliest aircraft were diverted for transport duties. Liberator I aircraft began to join Coastal Command in June 1941, being issued to No. 120 Squadron, then based at Nutts Corner, near Belfast. With an operational range of 2,400 miles, they became the very first VLR aircraft of Coastal Command and helped to 'close the gap' in the middle of the Atlantic where German U-boats had previously operated unhindered by shore-based aircraft. Later, in June 1942, a number of Liberator II (based on the B-24D) aircraft were delivered to Coastal Command. These had additional long-range fuel tanks and a further increase in range.

These were later joined by Liberator III and IIIA aircraft, the latter being supplied under the Lend-Lease arrangements. Later, these were supplemented by the Liberator GR.V aircraft, once again under the Lend-Lease terms.

From the middle of 1942, around 200 Fortress II and IIA aircraft were delivered to Coastal Command and began to enter service alongside the VLR Liberator aircraft. While not possessing the VLR capabilities of the Liberator, they did have a range in excess of 1,100 miles and made a significant contribution to the Command.

Finally, Coastal Command had equipment with which they could assist and protect the safer passage of crucial Atlantic convoys. It was to have a significant impact on the war effort.

Although first introduced into RAF service in 1936, the Saro London was one of the biplane flyingboat types still in front-line service with Coastal Command in September 1939 – with twenty-nine of the type on strength. In fact, two London flying boats were patrolling over the North Sea when war was declared. This photograph shows a London II, serial number K5910/BN-L, of No. 240 Squadron based at RAF Sullom Voe, in the Shetland Islands, in flight over the North Sea in mid-May 1940. (*Crown Copyright/Air Historical Branch image CH-1922*)

The Supermarine Stranraer was the last of a long line of biplane flyingboats designed by R.J. Mitchell. The type had made its first flight on 27 July 1934 and was followed by an order for seventeen aircraft. It entered service with No. 228 Squadron at Pembroke Dock in July 1937. At the outbreak of hostilities, fifteen Stranraer aircraft were on the strength of Coastal Command. This image, shot in 1941, depicts a No. 240 Squadron aircraft – serial number K7295/BN-L – operating from Loch Ryan. (*Crown Copyright/Air Historical Branch image CH-2551*)

Produced as a military development of the 'C' Class Empire flyingboat, the Short Sunderland I entered service with the RAF in June 1938, when it was a most welcome addition to the then limited airframes in use with Coastal Command. At the outbreak of the Second World War, three squadrons within Coastal Command were equipped with the Sunderland. This image shows a formation of Sunderland I (including L5799 and L5805) flyingboats of No. 228 Squadron, based at Pembroke Dock, approaching Newhaven on the East Sussex coast. The aircraft were still in their early all-over silver colour scheme and were painted in camouflage shortly afterwards. (*Crown Copyright/Air Historical Branch image CH-34*)

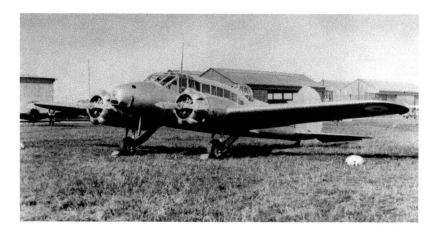

The Avro Anson was a military development of the Avro 652 six-passenger commercial aircraft ordered by Imperial Airways in 1934. The prototype military derivative – the Anson – made its first flight on 24 March 1935 and an initial order for 174 aircraft was placed. The first production aircraft entered service with No. 48 Squadron at RAF Manston on 6 March 1936. After 3½ years' service with Coastal Command, the Anson had just begun to be replaced by the first of the Lockheed Hudson aircraft at the outbreak of the war, but the Anson remained in service with twelve squadrons. This image depicts an Anson I, serial number K8828, in service with Flying Training Command at RAF North Coates at the outbreak of the war. (*Crown Copyright/Air Historical Branch image CH-138*)

The crew of a badly damaged Lockheed Hudson I, N7264/QX-Q, of No. 224 Squadron pictured on their return to base at RAF Wick from a sortie over Norway on 23 April 1940. N7264 was one of a battle flight of three Hudson aircraft providing long-range fighter cover for Allied troops in Norway. While flying over Romsdal Fjord they were mistakenly fired on by the C–Class light cruiser HMS *Curacoa*. One Hudson (N7249) was shot down and N7264 suffered severe damage to its wings and flaps, as well as two burst tyres. Despite this, Pilot Officer H. O'Neill managed to bring his aircraft back to Wick, where he made a safe touchdown. (*Crown Copyright/Air Historical Branch image CH-42*)

Sunderland I L2163/DA-G of No. 210 Squadron, RAF Oban, was photographed over the Atlantic while escorting Canadian Troop Convoy 6 (TC6), inbound for Greenock, on 31 July 1940. (*Crown Copyright/ Air Historical Branch image CH-795*)

The Fokker T.8W was a general reconnaissance seaplane used by the Royal Netherlands Navy. In June 1940, after the German invasion, five of these aircraft came to the UK and operated alongside Anson aircraft with No. 320 (Dutch) Squadron at RAF Pembroke Dock. The five aircraft were allocated the RAF serials AV958–965 and operated Coastal Command's convoy patrols over the Western Approaches. This image, taken in August 1940, shows one of those aircraft operating along the Welsh coastline. The remaining aircraft were withdrawn from service in November 1940, when they were replaced with Hudson 1 aircraft. (*Crown Copyright/Air Historical Branch image CH-1156/B.J.H. Daventry*)

A Lockheed Hudson I, serial number T9277/QX-W, was photographed returning from a coastal patrol in August 1940. This late-build Mark I aircraft only served with No. 224 Squadron and was later reported missing during a sortie over Norway on 9 December 1940. (*Crown Copyright/Air Historical Branch image CH-999*)

The Blackburn Botha was one of the new types of aircraft chosen for the re-equipment programme of Coastal Command, which was just about to commence when war broke out. The other aircraft were the Bristol Beaufort and the Saro Lerwick flying boat. Sadly, both the Botha and Lerwick were considered failures and withdrawn from front-line service after a comparatively brief period. The Botha was ordered as a general reconnaissance aircraft or torpedo bomber but was only employed on limited convoy patrol activities. Later, it was transferred to operational training duties. This picture shows three Blackburn Botha I aircraft of No. 1 (Coastal) Operational Training Unit, based at RAF Silloth, in December 1940. (*Crown Copyright/Air Historical Branch image CH-1902*)

An Avro Anson I of No. 612 Squadron from RAF Dyce was photographed while passing over a Royal Navy warship in early 1941, during a convoy patrol sortie. (*Crown Copyright/Air Historical Branch image CH-1920*)

The Consolidated Catalina I first entered RAF service with No. 240 Squadron at RAF Stranraer in March 1941 and played an important role in the Battle of the Atlantic. This image shows a pair of Catalina I aircraft (with W8406 nearest) of No. 4 (Coastal) Operational Training Unit, based at RAF Stranraer, which were photographed while moored on Loch Ryan in March 1941. (*Crown Copyright/ Air Historical Branch image CH-2446*)

As well as providing the backbone for Bomber Command's early offensives against Germany, the Vickers Wellington also played a significant role in Coastal Command's activities, particularly in the general reconnaissance role. Three Wellington IC aircraft, serial numbers R1410/KX-M, R1378/KX-K and T2541/KX-A, of No. 311 (Czechoslovak) Squadron, based at RAF East Wretham, were photographed on 13 March 1941. (*Crown Copyright/Air Historical Branch image CH-2265*)

During the early years of the Second World War, Coastal Command lacked a very long-range (VLR) aircraft capable of protecting the Atlantic conveys on their long ocean crossings. However, when leading American heavy bombers – the B-17 Fortress and Liberator – joined the RAF, their impact was significant with both Bomber and Coastal Commands. This picture shows Liberator I AM922 shortly after arriving at RAF Aldergrove, after an eight-hour ferry flight across the Atlantic in May 1941. Liberator I aircraft first entered service with Coastal Command in June 1941, being issued to No. 120 Squadron, then based at Nutts Corner, near Belfast. (*Crown Copyright/Air Historical Branch image CH-2985*)

The Bristol Blenheim IV served with thirteen squadrons in Coastal Command. Although the type was withdrawn from Bomber Command in August 1942, the type continued to serve within Coastal Command with distinction. This photograph, taken in May 1941, depicts six Blenheim Mk IVFs of No. 254 Squadron, photographed while flying in formation over Northern Ireland shortly after the unit's arrival at RAF Aldergrove. (*Crown Copyright/Air Historical Branch image CH-2992*)

While strictly part of RAF Fighter Command, these Hurricane I aircraft of No. 245 Squadron, based at RAF Aldergrove, were photographed shortly after returning to their base after a convoy patrol on 5 May 1941 while they were on detachment supporting Coastal Command activities. (*Crown Copyright/Air Historical Branch image CH-2682*)

First flown in 1940, eighteen Northrop N3P-B seaplanes entered RAF service with No. 330 (Norwegian) Squadron – a Norwegian squadron operating within Coastal Command – at Akureyri in Iceland, in June 1941, where they were used on convoy escort and reconnaissance duties until they were eventually replaced by Catalina flying boats. They remained in RAF service until December 1942, when they were declared obsolete. This image depicts a Northrop N3P-B, 22/GS-F, of No. 330 (Norwegian) Squadron in flight over the North Atlantic in October 1941. (*Crown Copyright/Air Historical Branch image CS-92*)

The role of the Hawker Hurricane during the Battle of Britain cannot be understated; however, the important contribution the type played with the Merchant Ship Fighter Units, which from 1941 helped to protect vital convoys from attacks by enemy bombers during the Battle of the Atlantic, is perhaps less well-known. Mainly converted Hurricane Mk 1 aircraft were modified to be catapulted from the decks of merchant ships. Hawker Hurricane I serial Z4936/KE-M of the Merchant Ship Fighter Unit is craned aboard a Catapult Armed Merchant (CAM) ship at Gibraltar in March 1942. (*Crown Copyright/Air Historical Branch image CH-6916*)

The Bristol Beaufort was Coastal Command's standard torpedo-bomber from 1940 to 1943. This photograph depicts a Beaufort I, serial number N1174, of the Coastal Command Development Unit based at Carew Cheriton and fitted with early ASV (air-to-surface vessel) Mark II radar, while undergoing trials at the unit. (*Crown Copyright/Air Historical Branch image CH-15217*)

A close-up view of the early ASV (air-to-surface vessel) Mark II radar aerials located on the underside of the fuselage. (*Crown Copyright/Air Historical Branch image CH-15219*)

The first Boeing Fortress IIA for Coastal Command, FK184, pictured shortly after arriving in the UK in March 1942. It is still carrying its American serial, 41-2513, on the tail. This version was equivalent to the B-17E model used by the US Army Air Force and incorporated several key improvements after the failure of the Fortress I aircraft used earlier by No. 90 Squadron. FK184 went on to serve with Nos 206 and 251 Squadrons of Coastal Command until it was scrapped in July 1945. (*Crown Copyright/ Air Historical Branch image CH-17922*)

The Armstrong Whitworth Whitley was one of the mainstays of Bomber Command during the early part of the Second World War. During the course of Whitley V production for Bomber Command, a special variant – the Whitley GR.VII, a general reconnaissance version for anti-submarine patrols – was also built. Later, Whitley V aircraft were transferred from Bomber to Coastal Command. This image, taken at Reykjavik, Iceland, in May 1942, shows two Armstrong Whitworth Whitley V aircraft (Z6968/WL-J furthest) of No. 612 Squadron, lined up beside the runway. The Air Ministry censor has annoyingly obliterated the ASV radar aerials atop the fuselage of Z6968. (*Crown Copyright/Air Historical Branch image CS-250*)

The Vickers Wellington first operated in a maritime capacity in January 1940 when they were fitted with a 48-feet-diameter electromagnetic Dural hoop for exploding magnetic mines. This version was known as the DWI (Directional Wireless Installation) and was very successful. This image shows a Wellington DWI aircraft of No. 1 General Reconnaissance Unit, flying south-west over the harbour at Tripoli during a mine-clearance operation soon after the occupation of the city by the Allies on 23 January 1943. (*Crown Copyright/Air Historical Branch image CM-5201*)

Boeing Fortress IIA aircraft at their dispersal points at Terceira airfield on the Azores in December 1943. Those nearest the camera are FL459/J and FK200/B of No. 220 Squadron. Also visible in this image is the construction of the steel plate runway under way in the middle of the airfield. After British-Portuguese negotiations had concluded, 'Force 131' landed in the Azores in September 1943 to set up an airfield for three Coastal Command squadrons, as well as a Transport Command staging post. RAF operations in the Azores finally ended in October 1946. (*Crown Copyright/Air Historical Branch image CA-1*)

With the limited range offered by both HF and VHF radio transmissions, particularly from low-level aircraft close to the surface of the sea while on convoy patrols, the importance of messaging with old-fashioned carrier pigeons should not be under-estimated! Multinational crewmen of Liberator GR.Va BZ818/C of No. 53 Squadron are seen handling containers of homing pigeons at RAF St Eval, after a patrol over the Bay of Biscay. Sergeant J. Knapp of Toronto, Canada, (in the hatchway) hands a pigeon carrier to Sergeant W. Tatum of London, while Warrant Officer A. Mackinnon of Auckland, New Zealand, holds a second carrier. (*Crown Copyright/Air Historical Branch image CH-12364*)

The Handley Page Halifax was the second of Britain's four-engine bombers to enter service with the RAF and, later, went on to serve as a general reconnaissance aircraft with Coastal Command; some entered service as early as the end of 1942 under the designation GR.II. Later, Halifax III aircraft were also transferred to Coastal Command. This photograph, taken at RAF Stornoway in February 1945, shows aircrew of No. 502 Squadron walking to their aircraft past other Halifax III aircraft. Despite being withdrawn from Bomber Command service immediately after the war, Halifax aircraft continued to serve with Coastal Command as the GR.VI. (*Crown Copyright/Air Historical Branch image CH-14814/B.J.H. Daventry*)

The last patrol! Short Sunderland GR.V ML778/NS-Z, flown by Wing Commander J. Barrett DFC, the Commanding Officer of No. 201 Squadron, and his crew, based at Castle Archdale, was photographed while undertaking Coastal Command's last operational patrol of the war, on 3 June 1945, escorting an Atlantic convoy south-west of Ireland. (*Crown Copyright/Air Historical Branch image CH-15302*)

U-boat Wars (1939–45)

A spectacular image taken from Short Sunderland III W4030/H of No. 10 Squadron RAAF while attacking German type VIIC submarine *U-243*, west of St Nazaire in the Bay of Biscay on 8 July 1944. Depth charges dropped by W4030, one of which crippled the U-boat, explode by its stern. Splashes from machine-gun fire from the Sunderland's rear turret, which put both the submarine's 37-mm and port twin 20-mm guns out of action, can be seen leading across the water below the depth charge explosion. After further attacks by another Sunderland of No. 10 Squadron RAAF and a US Navy Liberator, *U-243* was abandoned by its crew and sank shortly afterwards. (*Crown Copyright/Air Historical Branch image C-4603*)

During the Second World War, Coastal Command's most important contribution was probably the protection of Allied Convoys from attacks from the German Kriegsmarine's U-boat fleet. An Air Ministry publication titled *Coastal Command 1939–1942*, first published in 1943, explains, in its wonderful wartime language, the options available to Coastal Command in their war on the U-boat packs. By way of an introduction to this chapter, the opening paragraph of 'Chapter 10: The Attack on the U-boats' is detailed below:

> Coastal Command has, broadly speaking, three methods of dealing with a U-boat once it has left harbour and is on the high seas seeking its prey. It may be discovered by an anti-submarine patrol in the areas where these operate. It is then attacked by the patrolling aircraft and subsequently by others sent, in response to a signal, from the nearest base if it be within range. Such an attack is called a U-boat "strike". The enemy submarine may also be found by aircraft engaged on a sweep or a special search. This is the second method. The third is used when the U-boat is near a convoy. If sighted it will be attacked by the aircraft detailed to give protection to that convoy. A U-boat at large has therefore to run the gauntlet twice and perhaps three times on the way out and the same number of

times on the way back. Moreover, signals sent by an aircraft reporting that it has sighted a submarine are automatically picked up by other aircraft and by vessels of the Royal Navy. Any in the neighbourhood immediately proceed to the attack.

Perhaps, written during the middle of the Second World War, it may show a hint of propaganda and public assurance, thereby slightly understating the problems, as well as the significant threats, the U-boats actually posed to the convoys. After all, Britain relied very heavily on imported good, food, raw materials, armaments and, later, troops. Shipping losses to U-boats were high, particularly in the early war years and especially on the Atlantic convoys. Methods of hunting the U-boats improved significantly towards the end of the war, as did the weapons used to attack them; as a consequence, Allied attacks on the U-boats became progressively more successful.

At the start of the Second World War, the German Kriegsmarine succeeded in getting thirty-nine of their then fifty-eight U-boats out into the Atlantic undetected during August 1939. The Allies soon realised the U-boats meant business when they sank the SS *Athenia*, an unarmed passenger ship, on 3 September – the very first day of the war. The attack was in contravention of international agreements, and the British assumed that the destruction of the *Athenia* was the start of all-out submarine warfare and took the appropriate measures. In fact, Admiral Karl Doenitz, flag officer U-boats, had imposed strict controls, and the sinking of *Athenia* was 'a mistake', as the captain of *U-30* thought the vessel was an auxiliary cruiser.

Despite the poor level and quantity of equipment possessed by Coastal Command, their position at the beginning of the Second World War was relatively comfortable for the first nine months, the period known as the 'Phoney War'. Aside from those vessels that had left their home ports under cover of darkness and poor weather ahead of the outbreak of the war, the German U-boats initially had a particularly difficult task in getting from their home ports into the Atlantic hunting grounds as their primary route – through the English Channel – was heavily defended by the Royal Navy and the French navy, while the French navy was also responsible for covering around half of the Atlantic. When France fell in June 1940, the French protection disappeared while the German navy were now able to benefit from the use of the former French ports, with a gateway straight into the Atlantic, enabling them to pick-off the all-important supply convoys.

At the start of the conflict, there were large numbers of home-coming vessels approaching the UK, meaning many easy targets for the U-boats, who positioned themselves in the approaches. The initial results were grim, with forty-one ships being sunk, totalling around 154,000tons. In addition, the U-boats were able to pickoff the straggling, slower vessels in the poorly protected convoys.

Initially, the flying boats – mainly Sunderland aircraft – who were conducting reconnaissance sorties were also expected to locate the enemy surface raiders, while also co-ordinating with naval anti-submarine groups around the British Isles. It became immediately apparent that Coastal Command was seriously overstretched. Initial trials with Fleet Air Arm aircraft operating from aircraft carriers cost the loss of the *Courageous* when it was torpedoed by *U-29*, just three days after a narrow escape for HMS *Ark Royal*.

Further assistance for Coastal Command was requested and Bomber Command detached No. 58 Squadron's Whitley III aircraft to Boscombe Down to fly convoy escort and anti-submarine patrols over the western end of the English Channel.

By 13 November 1940, the location of and attacks on U-boats had been officially declared of equal importance to the search for surface ships, representing a significant shift in attitude from the Admiralty.

During January 1940, Air-to-Surface (ASV) Mk I radar made its first appearance in Hudson aircraft. It proved itself of immediate use in locating convoys, while in ideal conditions it could detect a fully surfaced submarine at a range of up to 3 miles, although it was incapable of locating a periscope or conning tower.

On 30 January 1940, the crew of a No. 228 Squadron Sunderland I aircraft sighted and attacked a surfaced U-boat which had earlier been depth-charged by convoy escorts. Unable to submerge and with aircraft and surface vessels in the area, its captain chose to scuttle *U-55* and it was officially part credited to No. 228 Squadron.

When Germany chose to invade Norway, it resulted in the temporary removal of all U-boats from the Atlantic, which in turn led to a significant reduction in shipping losses. In April 1940 Britain invaded the Faroe Islands and on 10 May invaded Iceland. This was not so much an act of pure aggression but rather a way of preventing the crucially located islands becoming ports of convenience for the U-boat fleet. It also allowed Britain to setup a destroyer and aircraft base for the British anti-submarine force. Initially, No. 98 Squadron with Fairey Battles arrived on 31 July at Kaldadarnes, on secondment to Coastal Command; they were all that could be spared at the time.

In June 1940, U-boats returned to the Atlantic and shipping losses increased considerably. In August 1940, Admiral Doenitz ordered a change of U-boat tactics and they started to attack individual ships at night – there being little chance of an aircraft locating a U-boat by visual means or by the use of ASV. In August 1940, Hitler declared a total blockade of the British Isles, stating that neutral ships would be sunk on sight. The following month, the Fw200 Condor aircraft operating from Bordeaux commenced long-range attacks on shipping. Aside from the aggressive firepower against single ships or stragglers, they could sit out of range of the defenders and provide excellent information to shadowing U-boats, enabling them to attack the convoys.

During October 1940, Coastal Command aircraft began to be fitted with the much-improved ASR Mk II radar, while also receiving improved depth charges along with short-range radio equipment enabling them to communicate with other aircraft and shipping without relying on the Aldis lamp.

The Consolidated Catalina arrived in Coastal Command service in early 1941 and replaced Short Stranraer flying boats with No. 240 Squadron at their Stranraer base. They were followed in the spring of 1941 by the first Very Long Range (VLR) Consolidated Liberator aircraft. Once sufficient numbers were in service, both would have a big impact on Coastal Command operations. The Liberator with its VLR capabilities was able to operate in mid-Atlantic where, up until then, U-boats had been free to operate without aerial intervention.

In June 1941, following significant shipping losses to U-boats, Winston Churchill approved an additional fifteen squadrons and while the equipment was not immediately forthcoming, it did mean the arrival of a number of ASV Mk II-equipped Wellington aircraft. However, the night attacks from U-boats continued, although a solution was in sight.

The Leigh Light

Following the circulation of a memo by the new AOC, Air Chief Marshal Sir Frederick Bowhill, requesting 'bright ideas', in an administrative office at Northwood, Squadron Leader

H. de Verde Leigh suggested the use of a searchlight fitted to the nose or under the belly of the aircraft. The scheme was enthusiastically endorsed by Coastal Command and the Leigh Light was put into production.

The Mk VIII Depth Charge Arrives

After eighteen months of war, Coastal Command was still very much on the defensive, and still to make a real contribution to the defeat of the U-boats. Up until this point, the special weapons that had been available for attacking both ships and, especially, submarines were fairly ineffective, having to drop them within a matter of feet if they were to cause any damage. The specially developed Mk VIII depth charge became available in quantity.

Defence Becomes Attack

Up to this point, Coastal Command had made 233 U-boat sightings, 164 of which had been attacked, although only one had been credited as a 'kill'; a further 25 U-boats had been assessed as 'damaged'. It was a sorry picture but the Command now had forty squadrons available to it, most of which had some anti-submarine capability. Effectively, with new aircraft, tactics and offensive weapons, it meant that Coastal Command had moved from purely defensive tactics to begin taking the offensive against the U-boat challenge.

Camouflage

In 1941, camouflage experiments had been conducted which tried to make maritime aircraft less conspicuous. The result was an instruction issued in August to paint all operational anti-submarine aircraft white on the undersides and grey on the upper surfaces – much like a herring gull.

By the end of 1941, shipping losses to U-boats had increased, as had the numbers of them. Germany now had around 200, of which eighty were operational, with half of them in the Atlantic at any one time. However, the Command's attempt to fill the gap in mid-Atlantic was seriously hampered due to the slow delivery of the VLR Liberator aircraft.

In early 1942, a squadron of Leigh Light (LL) equipped Wellington aircraft were delivered to Coastal Command as No. 1417 (Searchlight) Flight before officially being established on 21 February. With the USA now firmly involved in the war, Admiral Doenitz directed a number of his larger U-boats across the Atlantic to devastate the poorly protected US shipping along the eastern seaboard. And devastate they did, sinking forty ships in the first three weeks, totalling 230,000 tons.

In April and May 1942, more aircraft became available and the Leigh Light squadrons of Wellington aircraft were pressed into service; in early June, one of the Wellingtons attacked the Italian submarine *Luigi Torelli*, which was badly damaged. The first 'kill' using the Leigh Light came on 6 July when a No. 172 Squadron Wellington attacked and sank *U-502*.

A detachment of nine Lancaster aircraft from No. 61 Squadron arrived at St Eval on 14 July and were soon put to work. Just three days later, while on an anti-submarine patrol, one of the Lancaster aircraft spotted an oil patch coming from the conning tower of a U-boat. They dropped their entire weapons load of ten Mk VIII depth charges and two 250lb Anti-Submarine (AS) bombs in three runs. Shortly afterwards, the sailors of *U-571* were seen abandoning their vessel, which soon sank.

More VLR Liberators

After almost a year of operations five hard-worked Liberator aircraft of No. 120 Squadron had tried to fill the mid-Atlantic gap, but had only limited time on station. The Germans, becoming aware of the shortcomings, increased patrols in the area. The only real alternative was for more Liberator aircraft and a mission led by Air Vice Marshal J.C. Slessor went to Washington with plans to increase the range of the Liberator aircraft even more. The Americans were receptive but the aircraft was also required by the USAAF 8th Air Force, so delivery dates would be a problem.

Between July and October 1942, an additional LL Wellington, two Sunderland and two Liberator squadrons joined Coastal Command, while both Nos 206 and 220 Squadrons relinquished their Hudson and Fortress I aircraft for new Fortress IIA aircraft.

Code Breaking

By the end of 1942, Allied intelligence agencies managed to completely break the U-boat cypher code, although it occasionally took several days to achieve, and it was not always possible to route convoys away from the threat.

ASV Mk III

The German navy had already devised a system, code name Metox, which was a centrimetric radar warning device, to counter the ASV Mk II radar, which made detection almost impossible. The Allied response was to change the bandwidth of the new ASV Mk III radar, which was soon fitted to Wellington GR.XII aircraft which entered service with No. 172 Squadron.

Continuous Air Cover Over the Atlantic

By April 1943, the number of convoys across the Atlantic had increased considerably, as had the number of U-boat packs operating in their vicinity. The Germans had been able to crack the codes surrounding convoy activities and were being directed on to targets by German surface naval vessels. However, an almost continuous air cover was now being provided by the combined efforts of the Allies and to some extent the impact of the U-boat attacks was being mitigated.

When convoy SC129 attempted to cross the Atlantic with this almost continuous defensive top cover, the U-boat pack managed to sink two ships, with the loss of five U-boats however. Shortly afterwards, around seventeen U-boats attacked convoy SC120. During the next few days no less than six U-boats were sunk without any loss to shipping. During ten days in mid-May 1943, ten convoys, totalling 370 merchant ships, passed through the U-boat cordon, losing just six ships, of which three were stragglers. The strengthened defence tactics, particularly of the VLR Liberator aircraft, in addition to carrier-based Swordfish and Avenger aircraft, were providing a significant turn-around in fortunes. During May 1943, forty-one U-boats were destroyed, twenty-three of them by aircraft, causing Doenitz to order his 'wolf pack' to operate off the Azores, South America and the Caribbean.

Rocket Projectiles

In early 1943, the U-boat Warfare Committee had informed the Cabinet that Coastal Command had successfully completed rocket projectile (RP) trials, and in May Beaufighter aircraft of No. 236 Squadron were deployed to Predannack for RP operations over the Bay. The first success of this new weapon came at the end of May when *U-418* was sighted and attacked. Two RPs were fired in rapid succession, which were seen to pass straight through the hull, taking the U-boat straight to the bottom.

Additional US Liberator Aircraft

In June 1943, Slessor returned to Washington to make the case for further US assistance with the U-boat problem. This time, Admiral King was forthcoming and the 479th Anti-Submarine Group, comprising the 4th and 19th AS Squadrons (twenty-four Liberator aircraft in total), were despatched to St Evel, arriving in July.

U-boat Tally Increases

During the latter half of 1943, and despite changes in U-boat tactics, the aerial cover provided mainly by the VLR Liberator aircraft (some with the Leigh Light and the new Fido homing torpedo) was having tremendous success against the U-boat force, which suffered significant losses during the period. So much so that Doenitz had considered withdrawing his forces from the area – something he was eventually forced to do at the end of 1943. In addition, some Liberator aircraft also had RP capabilities in limited use, initially with No. 311 (Czech) Squadron, and had their first success against *U-966* on 10 November. The attack, conducted by a LL Wellington in conjunction with a pair of US Navy Liberator aircraft, resulted in the destruction of the U-boat after it beached near De Santafata Bay and was blown up by the crew.

Mosquito Joins the Battle

Towards the end of 1943, a new anti-submarine weapon was introduced when a Mosquito was fitted with a six-pounder (57mm) anti-tank gun in the nose of the aircraft. It was originally intended for anti-shipping operations but a number of Mosquito FB.XVIII aircraft and crews joined No. 248 Squadron at Predannack in October and were tasked with the anti-submarine role. The first contact with a U-boat occurred on 7 November when *U-123* was damaged near her home port of Lorient.

U-boats Return to the Atlantic

After bringing most of his fleet into port at the end of 1943 to allow numerous refits to be undertaken, including the new Schnorkel tube – which allowed the operation of the diesel engine and battery charging to be conducted at periscope depth – Doenitz could now muster around sixty ocean-going U-boats in the northern half of the Atlantic region. Opposing them, Coastal Command now had around 430 aircraft engaged in anti-submarine operations.

New AOC for Coastal Command

Air Chief Marshal Sir Sholto Douglas took control of Coastal Command on 20 January 1944 and soon moved to counter the threat of the large number of U-boats operating within the western approaches of the UK. In the first three months of 1944 alone, sixty U-boats were destroyed in the Atlantic, although fifty-four Allied ships were lost in the process. That said, it was just 25 per cent of those lost in the first three months of 1942.

In addition, a US Navy squadron of MAD-equipped (Magnetic Anomaly Detector) PBY-5A aircraft were added to the patrols over the Mediterranean, in company with Coastal Command Catalina (No. 202 Squadron) and Wellington (No. 179 Squadron) aircraft protecting the seas around Gibraltar.

Operation Overlord

U-boat sightings in early 1944 were relatively few in the Atlantic, partly due to the new Schnorkel tube, but it was also suspected that many were being held in French Bay of Biscay ports in expectations of the Allied invasion of France. The Allies believed the Germans could deploy up to 130 U-boats against any invading force crossing the Channel by drawing on those then operating in the Baltic and Norwegian waters. In addition, it was thought that another seventy could be at sea within two weeks of the start of Overlord.

A change in tactics was ordered by the AOC-in-C in April 1944 when No.15 Group would continue covering Atlantic convoys and, in conjunction with No.18 Group, cover the northern transit routes. No. 16 Group would patrol the North Sea and eastern Channel, while No.19 Group were handed the big job – the blocking of the western approaches. Coastal Command had thirty-six anti-submarine squadrons while additionally controlling three US Navy squadrons, eight Fleet Air Arm units and a single RCAF squadron. It was a formidable task but so was the U-boat force opposing them.

While U-boat activities did continue in the Atlantic ahead of Overlord, within twelve hours of the start of the operation, fifteen U-boats set sail from Brest, followed by others based at other Biscay ports. Thankfully, most of these were not equipped with the Schnorkel capability and during the night no less than twenty-two sightings were made; seven attacks were conducted, with two U-boats destroyed and four others 'damaged'.

During the night of 7/8 June, the thirty-six remaining non-Schnorkel-equipped fleet surfaced and fell foul of the Coastal Command Liberator aircraft. By 12 June, the German navy had lost six U-boats with a further six being severely damaged, which was enough for the remaining twenty-two craft not fitted with Schnorkel to be withdrawn from the area. However, during their return to the Bay of Biscay five were 'damaged' and another was sunk.

Sonobuoy and High Tea

To overcome the problem of trying to locate submarines under the water, the scientists had been working on the development of a 'sonobuoy'. Initial testing proved the system to work but production was slow to start and it did not make its debut until July 1944.

Meanwhile, in August 1944 the Germans were being forced to send their French-based U-boats out to sea, whether they were fit for operations or not, and it was no surprise that six U-boats were sunk during the month.

By the end of 1944, the German navy was about to launch two new submarine designs. The first was the 1,600-ton Type XXI U-boat, fifty-five of which were in commission, along with thirty-five of the smaller 250-ton Type XXII design.

At around the same time, the new 3-centimeter wavelength ASV Mk X had entered service and was not only undetectable by the submarines but also showed a significantly improved performance over previous versions – especially against the Schnorkel type. Meanwhile, progress with the introduction of sonobuoy receivers – codenamed High Tea – inside Liberator aircraft was progressing well. By the beginning of 1945, ten squadrons had been equipped with and trained on the new systems. However, it was not until March 1945 that the full weight of this new equipment proved itself – especially the effect of the sonobuoy – when a Liberator of No. 120 Squadron engaged and tracked an underwater target and then destroyed it with a pair of acoustic torpedoes, destroying *U-296* in the process.

Russian Advances

With the advance of the Russian forces, the U-boats were being forced out of the Baltic and they started running through the Kattegat in a desperate attempt to reach Norway. Much of these waters had been mined and many of the U-boats were forced up to the surface in an attempt to negotiate them, leaving themselves somewhat vulnerable on the surface. This allowed the Coastal Command strike squadrons – particularly Mosquito aircraft – to attack them, with a number of U-boats being destroyed.

Later, on 3 May, the North Coates Wing was active against U-boats in the Kattegat, with a mix of No. 236 and No. 254 Squadron aircraft attacking the U-boats, including the first Type XXI – *U-2524* – which was quickly despatched.

Shortly afterwards, attacking U-boats in the Kattegat became something of a slaughter. Thirteen U-boats were destroyed between 2 and 7 May alone, seven by Liberators, five by Beaufighter aircraft and a single U-boat by Mosquito aircraft.

Final Kill

On 7 May 1945, the final German U-boat sinking was accomplished when a Catalina of No. 210 Squadron spotted a periscope and attacked with depth charges. After continuing to track the damaged submarine using sonobuoy, a Liberator arrived to assist in the attack but still the U-boat evaded their attempts. A further Catalina joined the patrol, dropping four depth charges. Later in the day, *U-320* signalled that serious damage had been sustained and she eventually went to the bottom of the sea with no survivors.

On 9 May, Doenitz (as Hitler's successor) ordered all German armed forces to lay down their arms.

Coastal Command's U-boat Tally

Anti-submarine patrols and the escorting of convoys did not cease immediately at the time of the German surrender. There was absolutely no guarantee that U-boat commanders, many of them fanatically loyal to the Third Reich, would obey the order from Admiral Doenitz to surface, display a black or blue flag and, when contacted, proceed to a designated Allied port. Coastal Command had orders to take no chances. In fact, all did obey the order but it was a tense time and it was not until one minute after midnight on 4 June 1945 that Wing Commander J. Barret DFC, officer commanding No. 201 Squadron, received instructions to return to base, and that operational patrols had ceased.

Although more than a million flying hours were flown by Coastal Command crews on more than 240,000 operations during the Second World War, primarily seeking to locate and destroy U-boats, the number of submarines actually sighted, attacked and destroyed was relatively small. However, if one considers the proportion of submarines destroyed against the total number operated, the figure becomes more apparent – approximately one in five. If you add to that number almost as many U-boats damaged, crippled and forced to abandon their sorties to return to a safe port in order to undertake repairs, the ratio rises to almost one in three.

From 3 September 1939, Coastal Command had taken part in the destruction of 212 U-boats, and had sunk 366 ships with a total tonnage of 513,804 tons and damaged a further 134. The cost to Coastal Command was very high, losing 5,866 aircrew and 2,060 aircraft operationally.

The role of the Sunderland in convoy protection, particularly during the early part of the Second World War, cannot be understated, particularly in view of the number of German U-boats that hunted the convoys throughout their dangerous voyages to the UK. This image shows Sunderland L2163/DA-G, one of a pair from No. 210 Squadron, over convoy TC6 carrying Canadian troops to Britain on 31 July 1940. The convoy had left Halifax, Nova Scotia, on 23 July and was due to arrive at Greenock on 1 August. The vessel in the background which the wartime censor has circled for blocking out is the H Class Destroyer HMS *Highlander*. (*Crown Copyright/Air Historical Branch image CH-825*)

Another key asset in the fight against the U-boat was the Wellington GR.VII variant, which possessed the ASV Mk II anti-submarine radar. This image shows Wellington GR.VIII W5674/DF-D of No. 221 Squadron, based at Limavady, County Londonderry, at the Vickers-Armstrong Ltd works at Brooklands, Surrey, in July 1941, following its conversion from a Mark IC aircraft by the fitting of the ASV Mark II anti-submarine radar. This aircraft subsequently flew with No. 7 (Coastal) Operational Training Unit, also based at Limavady. (*Crown Copyright/Air Historical Branch image H-2359*)

The Lockheed Hudson was another aircraft used successfully by Coastal Command for convoy protection, particularly against the U-boat threat. This aircraft, a Hudson III with serial number T9465, was named *Spirit of Lockheed-Vega Employees*. It was famous as a 'presentation' aircraft, purchased for the RAF from funds raised by workers at the Lockheed-Vega Corporation, at Burbank in California. This image shows the aircraft being prepared for a sortie at RAF Wick in May 1941, shortly after being delivered to No. 269 Squadron. A clutch of 250lb bombs are being hauled into the bomb bay. The work of the wartime censor is visible in his removal of the aircraft in the background. (*Crown Copyright/Air Historical Branch image CH-2648*)

On 27 August 1941 Coastal Command claimed a rare and unusual success when one of its aircraft was instrumental in the capture of a U-boat. A No. 269 Squadron Hudson operating from Kaldadarnes in Iceland, flown by Squadron Leader J. H. Thompson, surprised *U-570* on the surface. Thomson dropped a stick of depth charges, after which the German crew was seen spilling out onto the casing, waving white flags. This photograph was taken later by a Catalina from No. 209 Squadron, called to the scene along with various Royal Navy vessels. Heavy seas initially prevented a boarding party from reaching the U-boat, but eventually they were able to accept the crew's surrender. (*Crown Copyright/Air Historical Branch image C-2062*)

FK185 was one of the first Boeing Fortress IIAs delivered to No. 220 Squadron, around December 1941, and was later selected for an experimental installation of the Vickers 'S' gun. This large-calibre weapon, sighted from the nose gondola, was intended to silence the anti-aircraft weapons when attacking a U-boat which had surfaced. The white distemper applied to aircraft of Coastal Command has worn badly and the aircraft's former identity (41-2514) can be seen on the fin. (*Crown Copyright/ Air Historical Branch image ATP-11675c*)

On 17 July 1942 *U-751* was attacked and crippled in the Bay of Biscay by a Whitley of No. 502 Squadron. This photograph, taken from the Whitley, shows the U-boat disabled, unable to dive and circling, apparently out of control. It was later attacked and sunk by a Lancaster of No. 61 Squadron, seconded to Coastal Command. (*Crown Copyright/Air Historical Branch image C-3143*)

An unidentified Armstrong Whitworth Whitley (probably a Mk VII) of No. 502 Squadron, coded 'YG-R', based at RAF St Eval, on patrol over the Western Approaches in August 1942. (*Crown Copyright/Air Historical Branch image CH-7050*)

On board a Whitley Mk VII of No. 502 Squadron during an anti-submarine patrol in August 1942. In the cramped cockpit the skipper consults with his navigator while the second pilot flies the aircraft. (*Crown Copyright/Air Historical Branch image CH-7048*)

Above: The Italian submarine *Reginaldo
Giuliani* was photographed while under
machine-gun attack from a Short
Sunderland of No. 10 Squadron in the
Bay of Biscay on 1 September 1942. Three
Sunderland aircraft were involved in the
action but were ordered to continue their
anti-shipping patrol before a concerted
attack could take place. The submarine,
which was sailing from Bordeaux for
the Far East, was attacked the following
day by a Vickers Wellington of No. 304
(Polish) Squadron and was forced to put
into the port at Santander, Spain, having
sustained severe damage and a number of
casualties. (*Crown Copyright/Air Historical
Branch image C-3333*)

Right: A Halifax II of No. 58 Squadron
caught this German U-boat, *U-266*, in the
Bay of Biscay while heading for the open
seas in late May 1943. (*Crown Copyright/
Air Historical Branch image C-3575*)

A peaceful scene at Castle Archdale (formerly Lough Erne) on 20 May 1943, as a seaplane tender passes a Sunderland III – serial number DD828/A, of No. 201 Squadron. Unfortunately, the wartime censor has removed all trace of the aircraft's fuselage-mounted ASV aerials! (*Crown Copyright/Air Historical Branch image CH-11075*)

A No. 220 Squadron Boeing Fortress IIA is seen 'bombing up' with depth charges at RAF Benbecula, on the Outer Hebrides, before a patrol in May 1943. (*Crown Copyright/Air Historical Branch image CH-11101*)

Boeing Fortress IIA FK186/S of No. 220 Squadron, based at RAF Benbecula, was photographed flying over the coast en route to its next patrol in 1943. (*Crown Copyright/Air Historical Branch image CH-11140*)

Another image of Boeing Fortress IIA FK186/S of No. 220 Squadron, this time flying low over the North Atlantic during a patrol in May 1943. (*Crown Copyright/Air Historical Branch image CH-11145*)

A posed image, taken in May 1943, of a radar operator flying on a Boeing Fortress IIA aircraft with No. 220 Squadron at RAF Benbecula working at his set, peering through a light filter at the CRT indicator screen, looking for the 'tell-tale signs of a surfaced U-boat'. (*Crown Copyright/Air Historical Branch image CH-18481*)

A number of Coastal Command Liberator II and V aircraft used by No. 311 (Czechoslovakian) Squadron were fitted with stub wings on the forward fuselage capable of carrying rocket projectiles with armour-piercing heads. Some aircraft were further modified with a bomb bay rack for the projectiles. This unidentified aircraft was photographed in June 1943. (*Crown Copyright/Air Historical Branch image ATP-MIS-LIB-43-1*)

An RAF tractor, towing trolley-loads of depth charges, negotiates a flooded dispersal area between Liberator GR.VI aircraft of No. 220 Squadron parked at Lagens, in the Azores, in late 1943. KG904/ ZZ-E stands in the background. (*Crown Copyright/Air Historical Branch image CA-109*)

Wellington GR.XIV HF197/1-D, of No. 172 Squadron, undergoing servicing at Lagens on the Azores. The squadron maintained a detachment flying anti-submarine operations from the Azores between December 1943 and April 1944. (*Crown Copyright/Air Historical Branch image CA-143/Fg Off H. Hensser*)

Armourers unload 250lb Mk VIII depth charges from bomb-trolleys beside a Consolidated Liberator GR.Va of No. 53 Squadron at RAF St Eval before loading them onto the aircraft ahead of another anti-submarine sortie. (*Crown Copyright/Air Historical Branch image CH-12373*)

A spectacular view taken from Sunderland III W4030/H of No. 10 Squadron RAAF, while attacking German Type VIIC submarine *U-243*, west of St Nazaire in the Bay of Biscay, on 8 July 1944. After further attacks by additional aircraft, *U-243* was later abandoned by its crew and sank. (*Crown Copyright/Air Historical Branch image C-4605*)

A German Type XXI submarine, *U-2502*, comes under cannon fire from a Mosquito FB.VI during an attack on four surfaced U-boats and an M-class minesweeper escort in the Kattegat by twenty-two Mosquito aircraft of the Banff Strike Wing. *U-2502* received only slight damage, but a Type VIIC submarine was sunk, a Type XXIII seriously damaged and the minesweeper left burning. (*Crown Copyright/Air Historical Branch image C-5338*)

The Vickers Warwick proved somewhat disappointing in its designed role as a heavy bomber with Bomber Command. Consequently, most of the early Mk 1 aircraft were equipped for Air-Sea Rescue duties and fitted with an under-fuselage lifeboat. The prototype GR.V variant, serial number PN697, made its first flight in April 1944 and entered service with No. 179 Squadron at RAF St Eval in the general reconnaissance role. It had a modified nose with a radar scanner beneath, carried a Leigh Light, and was equipped for anti-submarine duties. Its service life was short-lived, being replaced by Lancaster aircraft in 1946. (*Crown Copyright/Air Historical Branch image ATP-11818c*)

Swordfish III NF374/NH-M of No. 119 Squadron, on detachment at B83/Knokke le Zout, Belgium, was photographed at the start of an anti-shipping strike against midget submarine operations on 18 March 1945. The aircraft was still carrying its former No. 415 Squadron codes. (*Crown Copyright/Air Historical Branch image CL-2287*)

Above and opposite: Two images taken during an attack by Coastal Command Mosquito aircraft on German U-boats on 5 May 1945. One of the enemy vessels was sunk and the other damaged. (*Crown Copyright/Air Historical Branch image C-5361*)(*Crown Copyright/Air Historical Branch image C-5363*)

Anti-shipping Strikes (1939–45)

Mosquito FB.VI aircraft of No. 248 Squadron attacked a German M-Class minesweeper and two trawler-type auxiliaries in the mouth of the Gironde River, near Royan, France, on 12 August 1944. Bombs can be seen straddling the vessel, which later blew up. (*Crown Copyright/Air Historical Branch image C-4551*)

From the start of the Second World War, Coastal Command's primary objectives were both the protection of the Allied convoys from the German Kriegsmarine's U-boat force and to protect Allied shipping from the aerial threat posed by the Luftwaffe. Effectively, they had to defend the supply lines during the Battle of the Atlantic, as well as in the Mediterranean, Middle East and African theatres. At the outbreak of the Second World War they also had a maritime reconnaissance task – the 'endless chain' – patrolling the waters between Scotland and the south-west tip of Norway, through the most likely route used by the German navy to get their ships into the Atlantic. However, Coastal Command also had an offensive capacity, to strike hard against German shipping carrying war materials.

During the early part of the Second World War, Coastal Command's 'offensive' equipment was restricted to a limited number of Bristol Blenheim I and IV light bomber aircraft, in addition to a number of Lockheed Hudson aircraft. Early Blenheim I aircraft had been operating with No. 608 Squadron at RAF Thornaby, while the first Blenheim IV aircraft were delivered to No. 254 Squadron at RAF Bircham Newton in January 1940. The following month it was the turn of No. 235 Squadron at Manston to receive the Mk IV and by December 1941 a total of thirteen Coastal Command squadrons were operating the type.

Coastal Command's standard torpedo-bomber from 1940 to 1943 was the Bristol Beaufort, which succeeded the elderly Vildebeest biplanes in service. Beaufort aircraft entered service with No. 22 Squadron at Thorney Island in November 1939 and in April 1940 their aircraft made Coastal Command's first mine-laying sortie in the mouth of the River Jade, while on 7 May 1940, they dropped the first 2,000lb bomb. The Beaufort eventually equipped five squadrons in Coastal Command.

One of the earliest anti-shipping raids was conducted against the battlecruiser *Gneisenau* and the cruiser *Hipper* in June 1940. A force of twelve Hudson aircraft from No. 269 Squadron were sent to attack the ships, each aircraft armed with three 250lb semi-armour piercing (SAP) bombs and dropping them while flying in formation at 15,000feet. It was an early form of pattern bombing and while the cruiser was hit for the loss of two Hudson aircraft, the battlecruiser escaped damage.

Shortly afterwards, Hudson aircraft from both Nos 224 and 233 Squadrons attacked the *Scharnhorst* in the face of intense flak with little success, while shortly afterwards nine Beaufort aircraft from No. 42 Squadron at Wick, each loaded with two 500lb SAP bombs, attacked the same target – again, with little success. Sadly, four of the Beaufort aircraft were shot down by Bf109 fighter aircraft at they attempted to escape at low level.

On 24 June, Hudson aircraft attacked the *De Kooy*, claiming considerable damage, while earlier a 6,000-ton freighter had been attacked and set on fire off Kristiansud by a No. 220 Squadron Hudson crew engaged on an armed reconnaissance.

In May 1940, No. 217 Squadron had started the slow process of replacing their Anson aircraft with the Beaufort, but the squadron was still operating the Anson in September when it was detailed to bomb enemy aircraft in Brest harbour at night, a location with particularly effective defences. At this time, the new Beaufort aircraft were still being developed and were restricted to mine-laying or bombing sorties. Their use as torpedo bombers was delayed because the weapons were proving unpredictable at the higher dropping speeds required for the Beaufort. It was not until 11 September that a formation of five Beaufort aircraft was sent on a convoy strike off Ostend. Three torpedoes failed to release, another hit a sandbank, while one hit a 6,000-ton freighter.

By September, a co-ordinated raid involving six Beaufort aircraft of No. 53 Squadron, along with twelve Blenheim aircraft of No. 59 Squadron, attacked shipping in the harbour at Cherbourg. Of the five Beaufort aircraft that reached the target, one was shot down but the remaining four dropped their torpedoes, with a 1,600-ton freighter being sunk and a torpedo boat being badly damaged.

Shipping raids continued during the remainder of 1940, mainly against heavily defended targets, particularly against flak and fighters where losses were high. However, to make matters worse, the German navy's capital ships were continuing to plunder the convoys alongside the serious damage inflicted by the U-boat fleet. In 1941, Churchill issued one of his famous directives, giving the 'Battle of the Atlantic' full priority and ordering Bomber Command to concentrate on naval targets.

'Strike' Force

Early in 1941, the decision was taken to form a dedicated 'strike' force within Coastal Command, consisting of twelve squadrons equally split between long-range fighter, bomber and torpedo-bomber units. The four Blenheim fighter squadrons already in service were to be rearmed with Beaufighter aircraft; the three Beaufort torpedo bomber units were to be brought up to strength and another formed; and four Blenheim bomber squadrons were transferred to the force. The first operational coastal sortie was made by the force on 6 April 1941, involving Beaufighter aircraft from Nos 235 and 252 Squadrons.

Despite some setbacks for the 'strike' concept, the anti-shipping campaign was gaining momentum when Air Marshal Joubert took command of Coastal Command in June 1941.

The installation of ASV had begun with the Beaufort aircraft of No. 217 Squadron, then at RAF Thorney Island, but these were soon moved to Manston, where they formed the 'Shipping Interception Flight' – the unit being formed to use radar on moonless nights and during bad weather to find ships, then use flares to illuminate them and bombs or torpedoes to attack them, all assisted by 'Hurri-bombers' from No. 11 Group of Fighter Command. Sadly, the plan never really got underway and the aircraft returned to Thorney Island.

The six months between 1 July and 31 December 1941 had been a particularly busy time for the anti-shipping forces of Bomber, Fighter and Coastal Command. Their combined efforts saw 695 ships attacked; 59 were claimed as sunk (later verified at 41) for the loss of 123 aircraft and their crews.

Scharnhorst, *Gneisenau* and *Prinz Eugen*

Early in 1942, the battleships *Scharnhorst*, *Gneisenau* and *Prinz Eugen* were all under repair in Brest harbour, being closely monitored by British reconnaissance. With Hitler under the impression that the British were going to invade Norway, he instructed his admiral to move the entire convoy to Norway, where they could provide a stout defence of the country while moving them away from the almost continuous bombing attacks against Brest. Around the same time, the reconnaissance indicated that the convoy were going to make a dash through the English Channel and up the North Sea. Numerous offensive assets from across the Commands were placed on standby in anticipation of a strike against the vessels.

However, due largely to poor weather and equipment failure in Allied aircraft, the German ships made their way from Brest undetected. Eventually, the ships were located but only six FAA Swordfish aircraft of No. 825 Squadron at Manston, along with seven Beaufort aircraft at Thorney Island, were in a position to attack within two hours. A hastily arranged fighter escort for the Swordfish aircraft was put in place for what was a hopeless mission. All six aircraft were lost, along with thirteen crew members. Only four of the Beaufort aircraft at Thorney Island had torpedoes fitted and these were hurriedly prepared for a rendezvous with the fighter escort over Manston at 13:40 hours. The initial pair of aircraft was led to the wrong location, which was open sea, although the next three did make contact with and subsequently attack both the *Prinz Eugen* and the *Gneisenau*. Two aircraft later returned with damage while the third was lost with no damage to the ships. Frantic efforts were made by Bomber Command to launch an attack, with no less that 242 aircraft being launched, although most were unable to locate the targets and no hits were achieved by those that did. Despite numerous other attacks, the German vessels made it safely to their destination in the Norwegian fjords, where they now also provided a threat to the Russian convoys.

In May 1942, another large raid was launched against the *Prinz Eugen*, located near Stadlandet; but once again the result was the same: no damage to the ship but a large number of aircraft and crews lost. While attacks against the large capital vessels were unsuccessful, Coastal Command had much more success against enemy convoys in May–June 1942, although Allied losses remained high.

By September 1942, the Beaufighter had been confirmed as Coastal Command's principal strike aircraft and while deliveries were initially slow, they were arriving at squadron level – providing the 'strike' force with a little more aggression.

By September 1942, the German merchant vessels were running the blockade that had been setup by the Royal Navy with Coastal Command reconnaissance support, with trips from the Biscay ports to the Far East to collect valuable materials required for the war effort from Japan – rubber, tin and edible oils. Of the first convoy, five out of six vessels arrived safely. Sadly for the Allies, and despite considerable aerial attacks, the fortunes of vessels on their return journeys were similarly successful.

By the end of the year, the anti-shipping statistics spoke volumes for the poor return: just forty-two enemy ships had been sunk, with a total of 61,000 tons, for the loss of 251 Allied aircraft and crews. On 5 February 1943, Air Chief Marshal Sir Philip Joubert left Coastal Command under an undeserved cloud. He was replaced by Air Vice Marshal (then acting AM) J.C. Slessor.

Change of Direction

In order to counter the lack of anti-shipping success, a development of the integrated Strike Wing was devised. The new plan envisaged a force of ten Beaufighter squadrons, four of them torpedo-carrying with the remainder fighter/anti-flak units. It was hoped to have these operational by May 1943 with No. 16 Group operating from RAF North Coates and Thorney Island; No. 18 Group in the north at Wick, Leuchars and Tain; with No.19 Group at Predannack.

Unfortunately, the redirecting of aircraft to be deployed to the Mediterranean Theatre prevented it happening and anti-shipping successes for Coastal Command in the first six months were few and far between.

The First Major 'Strike' Success

In April 1943 things began to change. On 18 April, the Beaufighter Wing at North Coates was sent on its first 'strike' since the previous November. The target was a heavily escorted convoy which had left the Hook of Holland earlier that morning and was relocated off Ijmuiden by the crew of a No. 236 Squadron Beaufighter on a reconnaissance patrol. Nine 'Torbeaus' (the specially modified torpedo-bomber version of the Beaufighter) of No. 254 Squadron, six anti-flak Beaufighter aircraft of No. 143 Squadron, with another six from No. 236 Squadron, set off around 13:30 hours. Over Coltishall they picked up their fighter escort, comprising twenty-two Spitfire V aircraft from Nos 118 and 167 Squadrons, along with six Mustang I aircraft from No. 613 Squadron. The operation went almost entirely to the carefully prepared and practiced plan. The fighter and fighter-bomber Beaufighter aircraft attacked the escort vessels with bombs, cannon and machine-gun fire, while the 'Torbeaus' aimed for the freighters. Two M-class minesweepers were left on fire, while an armed trawler was hit. At least two torpedoes hit the *Hoegh Carrier*, a large collier, which subsequently sank. The entire raid was over in four minutes and no aircraft were lost – just slight damage sustained by two Beaufighter aircraft.

By April, the Beaufighter aircraft of No. 236 Squadron had bomb racks and the modifications required to carry 3-inch rocket projectiles (RP) – the latter proving to be a devastating anti-ship weapon, although special tactics had to be devised to maximise their effectiveness.

The Strike Wing repeated their performance on 29 April when two merchant ships and an armed trawler were sunk with the loss of a single No. 143 Squadron Beaufighter aircraft.

A similar Strike Wing had been setup at Wick and, on 17 May, conducted an operation under heavy fighter escort which proved another success. The first use of RPs from a Beaufighter was made during a detachment of No. 236 Squadron to Predannack, Cornwall, for anti-submarine work but by mid-June, all of the pilots of both anti-flak units in the North Coates Wing were well-practiced in its use, although it was not overly successful during an operation on 22 June near Scheveningen, when 176 RPs were fired against five Swedish vessels escorted by seven German flak vessels and five minesweepers. Two Beaufighter aircraft were shot down while four more were hit, with three of them crash-landing on returning home.

The faith in the Strike Wing principle was paying off and future raids continued with greater success and fewer losses, especially when the Strike Wing was accompanied by a heavy fighter escort.

After some serious high-level in-fighting in the corridors of Whitehall, planning went ahead for another two Strike Wings, although a shortage of suitably trained aircrew would slow their progress.

The first official attack by the Wick Wing was on 22 November, against a German convoy off Stadlandet, when six 'Torbeaus' of No. 144 Squadron, escorted by eight cannon-firing Beaufighter Xs of No. 404 Squadron, sank a Norwegian freighter and damaged two others for the loss of a single Beaufighter. Similar operations followed and by the beginning of 1944, the two squadrons were working well together.

It wasn't just the Strike Wings which were having increasing anti-ship successes; the remaining Coastal Command fleet, including Liberator, Wellington and Sunderland aircraft, were having their own joy in destroying enemy merchant vessels.

Another New AOC

On 20 January 1944, Air Chief Marshal Sir Sholto Douglas took over Coastal Command at a time when the Strike Wing had proved itself, and aircraft were becoming available in increasing numbers; just as importantly, air crews were also available to fly them. However, Operation Overlord was in the planning stage, in which Coastal Command would have a significant part to play.

In the first two months of 1944, anti-shipping activity was limited. One convoy was intercepted on 21 February when a merchant ship was seriously damaged, with other accompanying vessels also struck, but this was a rare opportunity. The *Den Helder*, a 6,400-ton merchantman, was located on 1 March and was damaged by RPs. Later in the day a large force of twenty-one Beaufighter aircraft returned to finish the job but it was finally sunk when a 500lb bomb dropped from a No. 415 Squadron Wellington finally finished it off.

German shipping would only now sail under the cover of darkness. Coastal Command's response was to illuminate the target with flares while a combination of Beaufighter, Albatross and Wellington aircraft would complete the task – the co-operation plan codenamed Operation Gilbey. The Albatross aircraft were on detachment to No. 143 Squadron, Coastal Command, and operated out of Manston.

Meanwhile, the Strike Wing at Wick was also having occasional successes, especially when they had perfected tactics using the 25lb solid head RP, which appeared to have superior flight and underwater characteristics when compared with the 60lb version.

The relatively new Strike Wing at Leuchars was not going to be left out of the action and on 5 March, Nos 455 and 489 Squadrons recorded their first combined success when sinking a submarine chaser off south-west Norway. The following day they successfully torpedoed a 1,000-ton vessel off Stavanger.

Up until now, the shipping-rich area between Ems and Elbe was out of reach of significant fighter cover – an essential element of the operation if it were to be successful. On 29 March, the North Coates Wing took a strong Mustang escort to the area and, with six 'Torbeau' aircraft, accompanied by ten rocket-equipped and ten anti-flak Beaufighter aircraft, they intercepted a convoy off Juist, north-east of Borkum. Two merchant vessels were sunk and the escorts badly damaged by a combination of RPs and cannon fire.

Ahead of Operation Overlord, Coastal Command flew operations in April with Albacore and Wellington aircraft aimed at securing the northern end of the English Channel while the Portreath Wing was taking care of matters at the southern end.

By now, an increasing number of FAA squadrons were operating in conjunction with Coastal Command, including a variety of Avenger and Swordfish squadrons. Operations on Channel Stop, Coastal Command's main invasion task, commenced on 30 April and it was not long before all of the General Reconnaissance (GR) squadrons were involved. However, the anti-shipping operations continued apace right up to and during Overlord. Once the invasion force was underway, the German navy tried very hard to interfere with the cross-channel supply convoys, so the Strike Wings were kept busy preventing them.

Mosquito Joins the Fight

By now, Coastal Command had the Mosquito in its inventory and both the FB.VI and XVIII variants were proving to be very fast and, more importantly, effective. On 29 June, during a combined Nos 235 and 248 Squadron operation, twenty-four FB.VI and two XVIII aircraft attacked a tanker and its six escort vessels. The tanker was left ablaze.

The Channel Stop campaign was so effective that German operations in the area were effectively neutralized. The Strike Wings were now completely on the offensive and looking for targets to destroy. The Admiralty decreed that all remaining vessels of the Marinegruppekommando West should be destroyed, so attacks were made on the harbour at Les Sables-d'Olonne, near La Rochelle. Here, the fast escort *Jupiter* was sighted and duly sunk by a hail of 25lb RPs. Another sweep by twenty-four Beaufighter aircraft of the Davidstowe Wing caught four M-Class minesweepers in Bougenelf Bay near St Nazaire. All were set on fire, although a single No. 404 Squadron Beaufighter was lost.

Political Changes

It was around this time that Sweden decided to withdraw its ships from German ports and immediately around 450,000tons of shipping was denied to them. Shortly afterwards, on 4 September 1944, Finland signed an armistice with Russia and another 363,000tons were no longer available to them. Then Sweden closed its ports to Germany and the pressure was piling on the Wehrmacht.

Further pressure was caused by the arrival of 100,000 troops in Norway, en route from Finland to Germany. All had to be moved by ship through Norwegian waters in order to return to Germany. With twenty to thirty vessels passing along the Norwegian coast daily, the Kattegat became a choke point and it became a very attractive target, although it remained a difficult waterway in which to attack shipping. Its distance from Scotland made operations difficult for the existing wings but in September 1944, Banff – which had been a training base up to this point – was cleared, allowing the deployment of No. 154 (GR) Wing. This consisted of two Beaufighter squadrons (Nos 144 and 404 from Wick), and two Mosquito squadrons (Nos 235 and 248 from Portreath). They made their first operation off Kristiansand on 14 September, when a coastal freighter was badly damaged and a flak ship sunk. On 19 September, a force of thirty-two Beaufighter aircraft attacked a convoy near Stavanger with the destruction of two merchant vessels and two days later a mixed force of eighteen Beaufighter and eight Mosquito aircraft attacked a small convoy off Lister, sinking a freighter while also damaging a coastal freighter. Operations in the region continued apace, with a good level of success.

Tse-Tse Mosquito

Coastal Command had available a very small number of Mosquito Mk XVIII from No. 248 Squadron equipped with a quick-firing (QF) 6-pounder, 57mm anti-tank gun in the nose of the aircraft. This version was known as the 'Molins Gun' after the weapon's manufacturer, as well as the 'Tse-tse'. The weapon was very effective, particularly against shipping. When Sholto Douglas requested an increase in the number of aircraft, it was declined as an RP-equipped Mosquito was under development. The first of these arrived with No. 143 Squadron at North Coates, replacing the Beaufighter with the unit. The unit was soon transferred to Banff and, after completing RP training at Tain, the first operational sorties were conducted on 26 October.

German Navy Withdraw from Norway

In January 1945, the German navy began withdrawing from Norway in anticipation of increased operations in the Baltic. It provided a number of targets of opportunity but a combination of bad weather along with difficult locations in which to attack prevented any significant successes, although a number of losses were incurred.

Planners at Coastal Command saw that a change in emphasis was now required, attacking laden tankers and merchantmen rather than small military vessels. Having suffered heavy losses during the January and February, No. 404 Squadron attacked a small Norwegian tanker on 26 February off Kristiansand, damaging the vessel. Later, on 7 March, the Banff Wing was once again busy when fifty-four Mosquito aircraft were sent to the East Skagerrak to attack a fleet of merchantmen escorted by a flak ship and eight barges. Four barges and the flak ship were sunk. The busy activities of both the Banff and Dallachy wings' anti-shipping operations continued. Despite this, and due to pressure in other theatres, the strength of Coastal Command was reduced in March 1945 by an anti-U-boat squadron and an ASR squadron, thankfully keeping the anti-shipping Strike Wings up to strength. This had been particularly important as operations in the period increased significantly for all of the Strike Wings – particularly over Norwegian waters and against shipping attempting to escape from the Baltic after the Russian advance.

The last anti-shipping raid was conducted on 4 May. One day earlier, a large formation of Mosquito aircraft from the Banff Wing returned to the Kattegat to attack the Penetration/Withdrawal patrol. The following day, they returned to the area when forty-eight Mosquito aircraft, escorted by eighteen Mustang fighters, attacked a seven-ship convoy escorted by an unusually strong force of flak ships. A merchantman was sunk and two others damaged. All sorties planned for 5 May were cancelled when it became obvious that Germany was on the point of surrender.

It was not the end of operations, however, as when most British-based squadrons of the RAF were celebrating VE Day, Coastal Command were still actively engaged on anti-submarine operations, which included a few of the Strike Wings. However, within weeks the Strike Wings were decimated when most of the squadrons were disbanded and the aircrew dispersed.

The Strike Wings had sunk 215 ships, totalling around 300,000tons – a significantly large proportion of the total German losses from air attacks during the period from November 1942 to May 1945 of around 450,000tons. A further 415,000tons of shipping was destroyed by air-dropped mines; although most of these were delivered by Bomber Command, some had been contributed by Coastal Command. By the end of the Second World War, the German navy had been virtually destroyed.

A pair of Hudson I aircraft of No. 206 Squadron, based at RAF Bircham Newton, flying at low level over the North Sea during a reconnaissance sortie by five aircraft of the squadron to observe the movements of German warships in the Helgoland Bight area in June 1940. (*Crown Copyright/Air Historical Branch image CH-314*)

Bristol Beaufort I torpedo bombers (including L9891/OA-F, L4481/OA-J and unidentified/OA-H) of No. 22 Squadron at RAF North Coates, preparing to depart for another anti-shipping raid on 19 July 1940. (*Crown Copyright/Air Historical Branch image CH-643*)

A Bristol Beaufort I, serial number L4516/OA-W, of No. 22 Squadron, waiting to be loaded with torpedoes ahead of an anti-shipping patrol from RAF Thorney Island in August 1940. (*Crown Copyright/Air Historical Branch image CH-1851*)

Bristol Beaufort I N1172/AW-S of No. 42 Squadron, based at RAF Leuchars, with another aircraft from the same squadron, photographed while en route for an anti-shipping raid in March 1941. (*Crown Copyright/Air Historical Branch image CH-2775*)

Three Beaufort I torpedo-bombers of No. 86 Squadron, based at RAF Skitten, near Caithness, photographed in loose formation at the start of an anti-shipping patrol in 1942. (*Crown Copyright/Air Historical Branch image CH-7948*)

Three Hampden TB.I aircraft of No. 489 Squadron RNZAF, based at RAF Skitten, photographed over northern Scotland while en route to an anti-shipping strike in August 1942. (*Crown Copyright/Air Historical Branch image CH-8653*)

Beaufighter VI.C interim torpedo fighter (ITF) JL832/A, of No. 144 Squadron, based at RAF Tain, on the side of the Moray Firth, in April 1943. (*Crown Copyright/Air Historical Branch image CH-9753a*)

The crew of a Bristol Beaufighter VI.C interim torpedo fighter (ITF) of No. 144 Squadron stand alongside their aircraft at a dispersal at RAF Tain. The Interim Torpedo Fighter, or 'Torbeau' as this version was known, was armed with a Mk XII aerial torpedo and an aerial camera port in the nose. (*Crown Copyright/Air Historical Branch image CH-9766*)

On 2 August 1943, Hampden torpedo bombers of No. 455 Squadron RAAF attacked a convoy off the Norwegian coast. This aircraft, L4105/D, suffered massive flak damage to its tail when half of the elevator was blown away, the starboard fin twisted and the port rudder fouled by debris. The crew were forced to lash a rope around the rudder bar and took turns helping the pilot, Flying Officer Iain Masson, hold the aircraft straight as they limped back to Leuchars for an eventual crash-landing. (*Crown Copyright/Air Historical Branch image CH-10730*)

A low-level oblique photograph taken during an attack on an enemy convoy north-east of Borkum, off the Frisian Islands, by twenty-nine Beaufighter aircraft of the North Coates Strike Wing. Smoke rises from a 3,000-ton merchant vessel which has just been damaged by cannon fire from one of the attacking Beaufighter aircraft. (*Crown Copyright/Air Historical Branch image C-4243*)

Sperrbrecher 102– a magnetic-mine detonating vessel – under combined rocket and cannon fire from Bristol Beaufighter aircraft (right and top left) before exploding and sinking during an attack by the North Coates Strike Wing on the vessel and its escorts off the Dutch coast, east of Ameland. (Crown Copyright/ Air Historical Branch image C-4312)

Armourers check the connections to a pair of 3-inch rocket projectiles (RPs) on the wing of a Bristol Beaufighter TF.X of No. 404 Squadron before taxiing out at RAF Davidstow Moor, ahead of another anti-shipping strike. (*Crown Copyright/Air Historical Branch image CH-13180*)

An oblique aerial photograph, taken by the nose camera of a Beaufighter of No. 236 Squadron while attacking an armed trawler with rocket projectiles, off the Frisian Islands on 18 April 1944; another aircraft of the squadron clears the target after delivering its salvos. Eight Beaufighter aircraft of the North Coates Strike Wing were returning from an armed reconnaissance mission when they delivered the attack on two trawlers, both of which later sank. (*Crown Copyright/Air Historical Branch image C-4376*)

A heavily armed German navy escort vessel seen from below mast height during a convoy attack by Beaufighter aircraft of the North Coates Wing off the Frisian Islands on 20 April 1944. (*Crown Copyright/Air Historical Branch image C-4314*)

Beaufighter TF.X NT950/MB-T pictured with D-Day-era 'invasion stripes' during its short time with No. 236 Squadron at RAF North Coates during the late summer of 1944. The aircraft joined No. 236 Squadron on 13 August 1944 but was hit by flak and abandoned off the Dutch coast just two months later. (*Crown Copyright/Air Historical Branch image H-1436*)

Mosquito FB.XVIII NT225/O of No. 248 Squadron, part of the RAF Special Detachment based at RAF Portreath, in flight on 5 August 1944. This version of the Mosquito, armed with a 57-mm Molins anti-tank gun mounted under the nose, was frequently referred to as the 'Tse-tse'. (*Crown Copyright/ Air Historical Branch image CH-14113/Fg Off Forward*)

A close-up view of the nose of Mosquito FB.XVIII NT225/O of No. 248 Squadron, showing the installation of the 57-mm Molins gun mounted under the nose. (*Crown Copyright/Air Historical Branch image CH-14111*)

On 12 August 1944, the *Sauderland*, a heavily armed mine detecting ship (Sperrbrecher), was hit off La Pallice by Beaufighter aircraft of Nos 236 and 404 (Canadian) Squadrons operating from RAF Davidstow Moor. The ship was left floundering and was later was finished off by the Royal Navy. The aircraft flying overhead the vessel in this picture is that of Wing Commander Ken Gatward, the Commanding Officer of No. 404 Squadron and one of the RAF's leading anti-shipping 'aces'. (*Crown Copyright/Air Historical Branch image C-4546*)

An oblique aerial photograph taken during a low-level attack on two German trawler-type auxiliaries south of Heligoland, by Beaufighter aircraft of the North Coates Strike Wing. A pair of Beaufighter aircraft can be seen clearing one of the vessels after raking it with RPs and cannon fire. This trawler was left burning fiercely while the other was torpedoed and blew up before sinking. (*Crown Copyright/Air Historical Branch image C-4639*)

Beaufighter aircraft from Nos 144 and 254 Squadrons, No. 455 Squadron RAAF and No. 489 Squadron RNZAF attacking – using RPs – German M-Class minesweepers escorting a convoy off the Dutch coast, north-west of Borkum, on 25 August 1944. Thirteen aircraft can be seen in the photograph, which was taken over the tail of an aircraft from No. 455 Squadron after delivering its attack. 'In an attack of this sort avoiding collision with other aircraft was one of our problems – and pilots needed to keep a very sharp look-out,' said Wing Commander Tony Gadd, OC 144 Squadron after the raid. (*Crown Copyright/Air Historical Branch image C-5169*)

RPs strike the 1,367-ton Norwegian merchant vessel *Lynx* during a successful attack by Beaufighter and Mosquito aircraft of the Banff Strike Wing at Stav Fjord on 19 September 1944. (*Crown Copyright/Air Historical Branch image C-4657*)

An oblique aerial photograph taken from a Beaufighter during an attack on shipping lying at anchor off Marsdiep – between Den Helder and Texel – Holland, on 25 September 1944 by the combined North Coates and Langham Strike Wings. The main target, the hull of an uncompleted merchant ship of 3,000 tons, can be seen to the upper right of the image, surrounded by minesweepers and auxiliary vessels which, with the shore batteries, were putting up an intense barrage of anti-aircraft fire. Three Beaufighter aircraft failed to return from the raid, while seventeen others were damaged. Against these losses, eleven vessels were sunk or damaged. (*Crown Copyright/Air Historical Branch image C-4661*)

The flak ship VP1605 *Mosel*, escorting the Norwegian freighter *Inger Johann* off Lillesand, engulfed in a torrent of fire from Beaufighter aircraft of No. 404 Squadron, one of which can be seen on the right of the picture passing at mast height. This attack was one of a series involving twenty-one Beaufighter and seventeen Mosquito aircraft from the Banff and Dallachy Strike Wings on 15 October 1944. (*Crown Copyright/Air Historical Branch image C-4944*)

A heavily armed merchant vessel is hit with RPs during an attack by thirty-one Mosquito aircraft of the Banff Strike Wing on shipping in the anchorage at Aalesund, Norway. Three vessels were sunk and one damaged for the loss of two Mosquito aircraft. (*Crown Copyright/ Air Historical Branch image C-5087*)

Ground crew manoeuvre a Fairey Albacore I of the No. 119 Squadron detachment into wind at B65/ Maldeghem, Belgium. The aircraft has been loaded with 250lb General Purpose (GP) bombs for a night anti-shipping patrol off the Dutch coast, probably in late 1944. (*Crown Copyright/Air Historical Branch image CL-1635*)

Four Beaufighter TF.X aircraft (including NV427/EO-L, nearest the camera, and NT918/EO-S) of No. 404 Squadron RCAF, based at RAF Dallachy, were photographed while flying in formation along the Scottish coast in February 1945. The following month, the Beaufighter aircraft were replaced with Mosquito VI aircraft. (*Crown Copyright/Air Historical Branch image CH-17871*)

Armourers fitting 25lb armour-piercing heads to 3-inch RPs and loading them onto the wing rails of a Beaufighter TF.X of No. 144 Squadron at RAF Dallachy. (*Crown Copyright/Air Historical Branch image CH-17876*)

A Mosquito FB.VI pulls out of its attacking dive over the Norwegian vessel *Lysaker*, after launching a salvo of RPs in the small harbour of Tetgenaes in Dalsfjord, Norway, on 23 March 1945. Twelve Mosquito aircraft of the Banff Strike Wing were involved in the attack, which left another large merchantman on fire and the *Lysaker* seriously damaged. (*Crown Copyright/Air Historical Branch image C-5117*)

An oblique aerial photograph showing Beaufighter aircraft of the Dallachy Strike Wing diving into the steep-sided Risnesfjord to attack a merchant vessel, the *Ingerseks*, moored by the cliff side. Smoke and spray from rocket projectiles fired by the photographing aircraft, and cannon fire from the other Beaufighter aircraft, have almost obscured the target, which was left listing and on fire. (*Crown Copyright/Air Historical Branch image C-5272*)

Air-Sea Rescue and Humanitarian Activities (1941–45)

A Sunderland flying boat of No. 204 Squadron rescues the crew of the *Kensington Court*, a grain-carrying tramp, which was torpedoed without warning on 18 September 1939, some 70 miles off the Scilly Isles. (*Crown Copyright/Air Historical Branch image C-1*)

It may seem a little surprising but at the outbreak of hostilities in 1939, there was no British military rescue organisation for aircrew forced down or abandoning an aircraft at sea. Instead, they relied on the Royal National Lifeboat Institute (RNLI), salvage tugs, any other vessels in the vicinity or, if they were in range, one of the high-speed launches (HSLs) established at flying boat stations.

New high-speed launches had been developed in the 1930s, with a range of around 500 miles, meaning no more than 250 miles from its base. However, at the outbreak of war, just seven were in service, dotted around the UK coastline. Aside from these, the rescue equipment carried onboard aircraft – life jackets, life rafts, distress signals, etc. – were of limited use and the quality on differing aircraft varied considerably. Some of the larger general reconnaissance aircraft carried dinghies and distress signals but most crews had little more than the Mae West inflatable life jacket, while others had nothing at all. Once again, Bomber Command took the lead in trying to remedy this situation and, following representations to the Air Ministry, another eleven HSLs were ordered. Another change that came about was in July 1939, when the responsibility for the co-ordination of searches was laid at the feet of the AOC of Coastal Command.

Following the activities in June–July 1940, there was a significant increase in the number of fighter pilot casualties; sadly, many of them drowned or were 'lost at sea' between the south-east corner of the UK and the Continent. It was this situation that forced the creation of a proper Air-Sea Rescue organisation. Initially, twelve Lysander aircraft were 'borrowed' from the Army

Co-operation Command to act as spotter aircraft, being able to drop a dingy down to them, before directing the HSLs or light craft of the Navy Auxiliary Patrol to rescue them. The results were immediately apparent and the twelve Lysander aircraft were retained on a permanent basis, under the control of Fighter Command.

The activities of this new – and successful – rescue service led to the setting up of a Directorate of Sea Rescue Services on 14 January 1941, who commenced their work on 6 February. They immediately set about devising methods of dropping survival equipment to downed aircrew, over and above the limited dingy drop already available with the Lysander. A number of methods were encouraging, in particular the Lindholme Gear. The first time this solution was put to the test was when rescuing the downed crew of a Whitley in April 1941.

Flying boats were able to alight on the open sea but the conditions had to be almost flat calm. Plans were made for the Supermarine Walrus to operate in-shore when conditions allowed, while the Short Sunderland had demonstrated its off-shore capabilities on 18 September 1939, when the crew of two aircraft rescued the thirty-four survivors of the SS *Kensington Court*, sunk by a U-boat around 70 miles west of the Isles of Scilly.

With the progress being made with air-sea rescue, the recovery rate of aircrew from the sea had risen to 35 per cent in June 1941, although it was felt that the organisation could do better. One of the problems hampering the activity was poor communications between the various parties involved so the decision was made to place the executive control of air-sea rescue more than 20 miles from the coast with Coastal Command. A new, senior executive, Marshal of the RAF Sir John Salmond, accepted the role of Director General and soon set about reorganising it. The old Fighter Command units were upgraded in both size and status with their operating range from the coast being increased to 40 miles in October 1941. They were re-designated as Nos 275–278 Squadrons, while for offshore ASR work, two additional Hudson squadrons (Nos 279 and 280) were established, with a strength of forty aircraft – many capable of carrying the Lindholme Gear, which consisted of five buoyant containers comprising a large M-Type dingy along with four ration and survival packs.

During 1942, the sailable dingy was developed into the Mk I Airborne Lifeboat. Initially designed to fit on the fuselage underside of the Lockheed Hudson, it underwent trials in July and the initial results were promising.

Warwick Joins the Fray

While the lifeboats, life rafts and dinghies were being developed, the Air-Sea Rescue service had a much bigger problem – an almost complete lack of suitable aircraft to conduct their missions. The venerable Anson was clearly unsuitable for the task, although there was little prospect of more Hudson aircraft, as they were in short supply. While the Wellington and Albemarle were considered, it was the Vickers Warwick that was selected for trials and on 21 January 1943, the Air Ministry announced the go-ahead with the ASR version to equip four twenty-aircraft squadrons. Despite slow progress, an order for 100 aircraft – designated the Warwick ASR.1 – was placed in May 1943, with a further instruction to convert forty surplus Warwick Mk 1 bombers into interim ASR standard, each capable of carrying two sets of Lindholme Gear. The Warwick ASR.1 completed its trials during July 1943 and aircraft started to arrive at squadron level. The final version – the ASR.1 Stage C aircraft – had increased fuel capacity, ASV radar and could carry either the Mk IA or Mk II lifeboat. By October 1943, No. 280 Squadron was up to a full strength of sixteen aircraft and became operational from RAF Thornaby.

Numbers of Rescue Craft Increase

During the course of the Second World War, numbers of rescue craft had gradually increased and by March 1944 had peaked at 182 RAF boats (130 HSL, twenty-five pinnaces and twenty-seven seaplane tenders); as well as seventy-eight Royal Navy vessels (fifty rescue launches, fourteen anti-submarine craft and fourteen rescue boats).

On D-Day alone there were 136 RAF rescue launches positioned within the assault area and during the first ten days of Operation Overlord 163 aircrew and sixty other personnel were recovered.

Meanwhile, new ASR bases were opened on the Azores and Iceland, thereby spreading the cover for Allied aircrew – both bases also provided a dual tasking capability with meteorological research.

Towards the end of the Second World War, a number of Lancaster III aircraft were converted by Cunliffe-Owen to carry an airborne lifeboat – as the Lancaster ASR.3 – however, the first of these was not available for delivery to No. 279 Squadron until September 1945, too late to see any action.

Post-war rundown

The rundown of air-sea rescue units at the conclusion of the Second World War was relatively slow. This was a sensible situation as there was no sudden cessation of aerial activities; in fact, the number of flights across the Atlantic in particular increased as a result of Lend-Lease aircraft being returned to the USA.

The first unit to disband was No. 282 Squadron, which was disbanded on 9 July 1945. It was followed by Nos 278 and 281 Squadrons in October, and shortly afterwards by No. 251 Squadron in Iceland.

By the end of the Second World War, a total of 10,663 persons had been rescued in ASR operations. These included 5,721 Allied aircrew, 277 enemy aircrew and 4,665 non-aircrew.

At the outbreak of the Second World War, the only means of rescuing downed airmen was a limited number of high-speed launches (HSLs) established at flying boat bases. These BPBC Type 2 'Whaleback' High Speed Launches, numbers 122 and 142, were photographed while at sea off Dover on 7 April 1941. (*Crown Copyright/Air Historical Branch image CH-2495*)

Gunners on board HSL169, a Type 2 'Whaleback' launch of No. 27 Air/Sea Rescue Unit based at Dover, man their twin Lewis gun positions on the afterdeck during an air-sea rescue exercise in the English Channel during 1942. (*Crown Copyright/Air Historical Branch image CH-7581*)

Photographed from a Hudson of No. 279 Squadron, HSL130 from Yarmouth, Norfolk, is seen rescuing the crew of a Handley Page Halifax from their dinghy in the English Channel on 9 June 1942. The Halifax crew had been forced to ditch after their aircraft incurred damage from anti-aircraft fire while raiding Essen, Germany. (*Crown Copyright/Air Historical Branch image C-2617*)

Designed as a heavier contemporary of the Vickers Wellington, the Warwick initially suffered from a disappointing performance. After being re-engined with a pair of Bristol Centaurus engines, the Warwick was ordered in quantity for Bomber Command. In January 1943, it was decided to convert a number of these into the ASR.1 variant, which was issued to Air/Sea Rescue units carrying an airborne lifeboat. This photograph shows a Warwick ASR.I, serial number BV403, with a Mk II airborne lifeboat under the fuselage. (*Crown Copyright/Air Historical Branch image ATP-11656c*)

An aerial view of a Warwick ASR.I, serial number BV403, which shows the under-fuselage Mk II airborne lifeboat in position. (*Crown Copyright/Air Historical Branch image ATP-11921d*)

Vickers Warwick ASR.I aircraft of the Warwick Training Unit (later the Air/Sea Rescue Training Unit) at RAF Bircham Newton on 4 September 1943. The nearest aircraft, BV277/T, subsequently served in the Mediterranean Theatre with Nos 284 and 293 Squadrons. (*Crown Copyright/Air Historical Branch image CH-18380*)

A Wellington GR.XIII, serial no. JA412/S, of No. 221 Squadron, based at Kalamaki/Hassani, Greece, photographed while in flight over the Aegean Sea on a humanitarian mission to drop relief supplies over isolated villages in Macedonia on 29 March 1945. (*Crown Copyright/Air Historical Branch image CNA-3535*)

The ground crew of a No.269 Squadron Warwick ASR.1 wheel a Mk II lifeboat to BV508/HK-B, at Lagens in the Azores, in April 1945. (*Crown Copyright/Air Historical Branch image CA-125*)

The No.269 Squadron ground crew then make the final adjustments to the installation of the Mk II lifeboat onto Warwick ASR.I BV508/HK-B, at Lagens on the Azores. (*Crown Copyright/ Air Historical Branch image CA-127*)

Above: Vickers Warwick ASR.I BV356/HK-E of No. 269 Squadron, based at Lagens on the Azores, photographed while in flight over Terceira in April 1945. BV356 was a re-designated 'Stage C' aircraft, seen here carrying a Mk II lifeboat. (*Crown Copyright/ Air Historical Branch image CA-129*)

Right: A Hudson III air-sea rescue aircraft of No. 520 Squadron flies over HSL181 of No. 71 Air/Sea Rescue Marine Craft Unit while returning to Gibraltar following a search in the Mediterranean on 2 April 1945. (*Crown Copyright/ Air Historical Branch image CNA-4710/ Flt Lt B.J. Daventry*)

Meteorological Research and Photographic Reconnaissance

A No.544 Squadron Mosquito PR.XVI, NS502/M, in flight from RAF Benson in December 1944. (*Crown Copyright/Air Historical Branch image CH-14262*)

Many pilots (the author included) consider meteorology something of an inexact science, or perhaps even a black art. However, its role throughout the Second World War was absolutely crucial. The first RAF Meteorological Flight was founded at Eastchurch on 1 November 1924 but was moved to Duxford in January 1925, when it was equipped with Sopwith Snipe aircraft. It moved to Mildenhall in 1936 as a 'lodger' unit at the Bomber Command station. The same month, a similar unit was formed at Aldergrove and made the first Temperature and Humidity (THUM) sortie in January 1937. Both 'Met' Flights received Gloster Gauntlets in July 1937, with Gloster Gladiators replacing most of them in May 1939.

The daily THUM flights provided useful information but as most weather systems approached the UK from the west, and in order to build up a complete synoptic picture for the whole of the UK, the Meteorological Office relied on weather ships positioned in the Atlantic. The system had worked well in peacetime but with the outbreak of war reports became virtually non-existent.

The Meteorological Office proposed that a series of THUM flights could be setup around the UK but while the Air Ministry understood the need for a specialist unit, the request was 'out of the question' – there were not even sufficient aircraft or crews available for offensive operations – although that viewpoint was about to change.

Following the fall of France in 1940, Bomber Command became increasingly anxious about the accuracy of forecasts generally, and in particular those concerning landing conditions for the aircraft returning to their bases. When strong representations were made to the Air Ministry, the Meteorological Office repeated their earlier case. Accordingly, three new flights –

Nos 403, 404 and 405 – were formed, while the THUM flights at Mildenhall and Aldergrove were re-designated Nos 401 and 402 Flights.

On 1 March 1941, Coastal Command assumed responsibility for all five Met units and they were promptly re-designated Nos 1401–1405 Flights. In August, No. 1406 Flight was formed at Wick when a small number of Hudson aircraft became available for their use. No. 1401 (Met) Flight moved to Bircham Newton and received Hurricane aircraft in order to achieve the altitude required on THUM flights, although these aircraft were replaced by Spitfire aircraft in 1942. Two additional units – No. 1407 Flight at Reykjavik and No. 1408 at Wick – were formed in the autumn, but as suitable aircraft were not then available, both units had to wait until April 1942 to receive their Hudson aircraft.

However, despite the amazing dedication to duty shown by the brave meteorological pilots, Bomber Command was unhappy and pressed for their own Met aircraft. At the end of 1943, they got their own way and the Mosquito Flight of No. 521 Squadron joined No. 8 (Pathfinder) Group as No. 1409 (Met) Flight.

When it was realised that more suitable aircraft, with a longer range, were required for the Met flights, a major re-equipment programme was undertaken. The Halifax V was selected as the long-range (1,400nm) aircraft, while the Ventura was picked for medium-range (1,000nm) work. Considerable modifications were required to allow the Halifax V aircraft to undertake meteorological reconnaissance and this work was completed by Cunliffe Owen at Eastleigh.

In August 1943, Nos 517 and 529 Squadrons (consolidated and renumbered from 1404 and 1406/8 Flights) were supplemented with a detachment of four USAAF B-17F Fortress aircraft at St Eval.

In Iceland, No. 1407 Flight had crashed all three of their Hudson aircraft by late 1943 and these were replaced by Hampden aircraft, but they were not overly successful in the harsh conditions, so three long-range Hudson aircraft were transferred into the unit. Equipment in use with the Met flights in 1943 and '44 became a fluid situation, with a variety of Halifax III and V, Ventura, Spitfire, Hurricane and, later, Warwick aircraft participating; at times they were supported by the USAAF's 8th Weather Reconnaissance Squadron in and around Gibraltar and the Azores. Later, the Halifax III and Fortress aircraft also carried depth charges to attack U-boats sighted during the weather reconnaissance missions.

Towards the end of the Second World War the remaining Met squadrons – four in the UK, one at Gibraltar and No. 269 (Composite) Squadron – continued to operate until most of the Atlantic ferrying was complete. Then, all but No. 518 Squadron quickly faded into history.

Photographic Reconnaissance

Aerial photographic reconnaissance has been around as long as the RAF has been in existence, having made significant improvements during the latter years of the First World War. Hugh Trenchard, the Chief of the Air Staff (CAS) for many inter-war years, recognised the importance of the aerial photography but as he hated specialisation of any kind, felt that any observer 'could operate a camera when required'.

In January 1937, the Deputy Chief of the Air Staff (DCAS) announced that 'we must regard the development of long-range photography as highly important and accord it a high degree of priority in research, development and training'. However, despite the words, progress within the RAF was painfully slow.

Some early photographic reconnaissance had been conducted in Germany, southern Italy and North Africa by a 'private organisation' run by an Australian individual – A.S. Cotton – which was basically a front for the Air Ministry.

By the summer of 1939, Blenheim squadrons within No. 2 Group of Bomber Command had been given a photo-reconnaissance role, while plans for the British Expeditionary Force to France included two similar units. In October 1939, a specialist photographic reconnaissance unit was setup under Fighter Command, with Spitfire aircraft as the equipment of choice. However, following the German breakthrough into France and considerable 'discussions' within the corridors of the Air Ministry, the decision was taken to place the role of photographic reconnaissance under Coastal Command, which was completed on 18 June 1940. The scope of the task was vast, as it seems that everyone had now discovered the value of aerial photography.

The new Photographic Reconnaissance Unit (PRU) was created, with an interpretation headquarters continuing at Wembley at the Photographic Intelligence Unit (PIU).

The threat of a seaborne invasion of the UK launched from anywhere on a 2,000-mile Continental coastline provided the PRU with its first priority. Thirty specially modified Spitfire aircraft (known as 'Bowser' wings), with special long-range fuel tanks permitting 1,750-mile round trips, were ordered; however, the limited equipment then available made the immediate task of the PRU a particularly difficult one.

The Germans were aware of the PRU's activities and made several attacks on their bases at Heston and St Eval. Accordingly, in October 1940, the decision was taken to move the operation to RAF Benson, where it was considered to be 'less vulnerable'.

'Dicer' Sorties

Soon, low-level operations were being introduced, as were a small number of lightly armed PR Spitfire aircraft. The low-level flights soon became known as 'Dicer' flights – as in dicing with death. In addition, a high level of navigational skill was also a priority as usually only a single pass over a heavily defended target would be permitted if the essential element of surprise was to be maintained.

Mosquito PR.1

The production version of the 'Bowser' wing Spitfire, the PR.IV, arrived in March 1941 and entered service early in the following month. The type was painted in a number of experimental colours before the use of cerulean blue (known as PR blue) was accepted. The new aircraft were soon demonstrating their capabilities and returned with some spectacular images.

By September 1941, the operational strength of No. 1 PRU (now a combination of Nos 1 and 3 PRU) was thirty-seven Spitfires, two Marylands and two of the new Mosquito PR.1 aircraft (including W4051/LY-U – see page 95 (top) for illustration). The prototype Mosquito PR.1 was the third prototype of the Mosquito ordered and made its first flight on 10 June 1941. A further ten Mosquito PR.1 aircraft were ordered for photo-reconnaissance duties. On the Mosquito's first operational sortie over Brest – made by W4055 on 20 September 1941 – the Mosquito was chased by three Me109 aircraft but completely outpaced them at 23,000feet.

The first Mosquito PR.IV was delivered to the PRU in April 1942 but further deliveries were slow and it was July before a permanent detachment of three aircraft could be placed at Leuchars, covering long-range flights to Norway and the Baltic. In the summer of 1942, the PRU had expanded considerably and now comprised eight Flights with more than seventy aircraft. By December 1942, No. 1 PRU at Benson were despatching as many as ten sorties a day and the long-range Mosquito aircraft were flying as far afield as Narvik in the north and the Skoda Works at Pilsen in the south.

In October 1942, the PRU was divided into squadrons – No. 540 Squadron at Leuchars, the six Spitfire Flights became Nos 541, 542 and 543 Squadrons, with No. 544 Squadron being formed to undertake the specialised night photography role.

By now the unarmed Spitfire PR.IV was being intercepted by Luftwaffe fighter aircraft, aided by improved performance and better ground radar. An updated version, the Spitfire PR.IX, was introduced, reaching No. 541 Squadron at the end of November 1942. It was followed by the Spitfire PR.XI, which was faster and could fly higher than most opposition fighter aircraft.

That was all fine until 25 July 1944, when a new Mosquito XIV of No. 544 Squadron was intercepted by a Me262 jet fighter over Munich. However, the manoeuvrability of the Mosquito allowed the aircraft to return safely. The following month, four PRU Spitfires were similarly intercepted by Me262 aircraft and one of them was shot down.

The AOC-in-C of Coastal Command had called for pressurised-cabin Spitfire aircraft to be introduced as soon as possible but deliveries were not made until November 1944, when altitudes of 42,000feet became the norm. The Mosquito PR.34, which had a proposed ceiling of 43,000feet, was also expected to solve the jet-interception problems but was delayed and did not enter RAF service until after the conclusion of the Second World War although it did go on to form the backbone of post-war RAF activities.

It should be remembered that the photo reconnaissance units played a key role during the Second World War – including the photography and identification of numerous vessels including the *Tirpitz, Bismarck, Prinz Eugen, Scharnhorst* and *Gneisenau*. Then there were the many Freya early-warning radar sites along with the associated Wurzburg azimuth and height-finding radar; the initial reconnaissance and later damage assessment images of the Sorpe and Eder dams; a link between the experimental station at Peenamünde and the numerous 'ski' sites in France; the later Crossbow sites in France; and photographic reconnaissance ahead of Operation Market Garden in 1944. Photographic reconnaissance had clearly proved itself during the Second World War. However, at the conclusion of hostilities, many of the PR aircraft, including various Spitfire types, were engaged on survey work, before being finally disbanded.

An airman topping up a psychrometer before fitting it under the wing of a Hurricane aircraft for a morning weather reconnaissance flight from RAF Mildenhall in May 1941. (*Crown Copyright/Air Historical Branch image CH-2723*)

Left: Civilian staff of the RAF Meteorological Flight, based at Mildenhall, plotting synoptic charts using the data obtained from the morning's reconnaissance flight in May 1941. (*Crown Copyright/Air Historical Branch image CH-2726*)

Below: The ground crew of No. 1401 (Meteorological) Flight guide a Gladiator out to the runway at RAF Bircham Newton for a meteorological reconnaissance flight in 1942. (*Crown Copyright/Air Historical Branch image CH-4027*)

Above: Members of No. 1401 (Meteorological) Flight pose with one of their Gladiator aircraft at Bircham Newton in early 1942. (*Crown Copyright/Air Historical Branch image CH-4029*)

Right: A member of the ground crew hands a psychrometer to meteorological pilot Flying Officer J.B. Gordon of No. 521 Squadron in Gladiator II N5897 'E' before he departed on a high-altitude THUM (Temperature and Humidity) flight from RAF Bircham Newton on 16 January 1943. (*Crown Copyright/Air Historical Branch image CH-18063*)

Mosquito PR.IX ML897/D, of No. 1409 (Meteorological) Flight (then part of Bomber Command), based at RAF Wyton as part of the Pathfinder Force, was photographed in flight in November 1944. All Met research was later transferred to Coastal Command. (*Crown Copyright/Air Historical Branch image CH-14467*)

Fortress Mark IIA FK197, outside the Scottish Aviation workshops at Prestwick, where it was being fitted with special wireless equipment. This aircraft eventually served as a GR.IIA with No. 251 Squadron, which undertook meteorological reconnaissance flights from Reykjavik, Iceland, in late 1945. (*Crown Copyright/Air Historical Branch image CH-6885*)

The first production Mosquito PR.I, W4051/LY-U, of No. 1 Photographic Reconnaissance Unit, RAF Benson, on 12 April 1942. (*Crown Copyright/Air Historical Branch image CH-18306*)

Spitfire PR.XI EN343/E of No. 542 Squadron, based at RAF Benson, in October 1943. (*Crown Copyright/Air Historical Branch image CH-18480*)

Supermarine Spitfire PR.XI PL775/A of No. 541 Squadron, based at Benson, was photographed as it flew over the photographer's aircraft, clearly showing the 'split-pair' camera ports under the fuselage, aft of the wing roots. (*Crown Copyright/Air Historical Branch image CH-13491*)

Another view of Spitfire PR.XI PL775/A of No. 541 Squadron, taken on 13 July 1944. The aircraft was delivered new to Benson on 22 April 1944 and allocated to No. 541 Squadron on 14 May. The aircraft was withdrawn from RAF service on 8 September 1945 and struck off charge on 7 April 1946. (*Crown Copyright/Air Historical Branch image CH-13492*)

Above and below: A No. 544 Squadron Mosquito PR.XVI, NS502/M, photographed in flight from RAF Benson in December 1944. The under-fuselage camera ports are evident in this view of the aircraft as it banks away from the camera. The arrangement shows a typical fit for high altitude reconnaissance, consisting of a vertical 'split pair' of F24 (14in.) cameras in the bomb bay, a further 'split pair' of F52s (20 or 36in.) further along the centreline with a single, port-facing oblique F24 in between. (*Crown Copyright/Air Historical Branch image CH-14263*)(*Crown Copyright/Air Historical Branch image CH-14264*)

Post-war Coastal Command Activities (1946–59)

Shackleton MR.2 WR960/X of No. 228 Squadron, on a sortie near its home base at RAF St Eval in 1958. WR960 was later converted to AEW.2 configuration in 1971 and served with No. 8 Squadron at RAF Lossiemouth. It was withdrawn from service in 1982 and at the time of writing was preserved in the Museum of Science and Industry in Manchester. (*Crown Copyright/Air Historical Branch image T-326*)

After the cessation of hostilities in May 1945, Coastal Command suffered an immediate and rapid rundown. Much of this was due to the terms of the Lend-Lease Agreements that had been in place with the US Government. It meant the immediate disbandment of all Catalina squadrons, while Boeing B-17 Fortress and Consolidated Liberator aircraft supplied under Lend-Lease were also returned to the US. The remaining Liberators that had been purchased by the British Government were handed over to Bomber Command. To make matters worse, most, if not all, of the Commonwealth personnel that had been serving with squadrons were immediately recalled home, which had a particularly major impact on the Sunderland force. Overall, Coastal Command was decimated.

The Short Sealand and Seaford aircraft had been considered, and then rejected, as replacements for the Liberator aircraft but to make matters worse, the Air Ministry had not placed any orders for equipment to replace the Lend-Lease aircraft. In particular, the replacement for the Liberator – a proposed new maritime version of the Avro Lincoln – was desperately required. As a consequence, the Short Sunderland had to continue in service until a new 'boat' could be found. One option would be to purchase outright some of the Lend-Lease Liberator aircraft, but that proved far too costly so, to fill the gap, modified Avro Lancaster aircraft, already destined to replace the Warwick in the ASR role, were procured.

In order to maintain something resembling a workable Order of Battle, numerous flights and squadrons were consolidated, while the operations were concentrated on a smaller number of airfields. Then, in 1948, came Operation Plainfare.

The Berlin Airlift

What started on 28 June as a joint British/US transport aircraft operation soon involved Coastal Command. Flying boats were the only aircraft with internal anti-corrosion treatment as a result of their waterborne operations – meaning that Sunderland aircraft would be able to transport the bulk salt that the normal transport aircraft were unable to carry.

On 3 July 1948, Sunderland aircraft from Nos 201 and 230 Squadron started to leave their Calshot base en route to the Blohm & Voss shipyard at Finkenwerder, near Hamburg, together with aircraft from No. 235 OCU. The first sortie to Havel See, a lake within Berlin, was flown on 5 July. Initially operations were painfully slow until a 30,000-gallon tanker barge became available. By 13 July, and despite the departure of No. 235 OCU on a detachment, the daily sortie rate had risen to sixteen and it continued to rise as turn-around times were reduced. Each Sunderland was able to carry around 4 tons of supplies – mainly salt and potatoes – and brought out manufactured goods and refugees.

The Sunderland aircraft continued to operate until 12 December, when the trips were stopped, due mainly to safety issues (uncharted sandbanks and wreckage which, in some cases, had been deliberately placed there by the Soviet forces to prevent operations) and the deteriorating winter weather conditions. However, over 1,000 sorties had been flown, carrying more than 4,500 tons of supplies, while evacuating 1,113 refugees – mainly children.

Stop-gap Neptune

While the RAF was awaiting delivery of the Shackleton MR.1, there was an urgent requirement for an aircraft to fill the maritime reconnaissance gap. Consequently, fifty-two Neptune MR.1 aircraft were provided by the US under the Mutual Defence Air Programme (MDAP). On 13 January 1952, the first aircraft (WX493) arrived at St Eval and on 27 January 1952, the first two aircraft (WX493 and WX494) entered service with No. 217 Squadron. Similar to the US Navy's Lockheed P2V-5, it operated with four squadrons within Coastal Command, at both St Eval and Kinloss, until the Shackleton entered service. All of the Neptune aircraft were returned to the US in 1957.

Shackleton MR.1 Joins an Expanding Coastal Command

The Shackleton was developed from the Avro Lincoln III, a projected anti-submarine reconnaissance version of the bomber. It retained the Lincoln's wing and undercarriage but introduced a shortened, redesigned fuselage. It was powered by four Rolls-Royce Griffon engines, each with six-blade, contra-rotating propellers. The prototype Shackleton MR.1 (VW126) made its first flight on 9 March 1949 and differed from later production aircraft in having a pair of 20mm guns in the nose and tail turret, in addition to the dorsal turret. Two further prototypes were built (VW131 and VW135) before production commenced with VP254, which made its first flight on 24 October 1950.

Seventy-seven Shackleton MR.1 and MR.1A aircraft were built and the first Shackleton MR.1 entered service in April 1951 with No. 120 Squadron at RAF Kinloss. Generally, Shackleton aircraft superseded Lancaster MR.3s in service, as well as equipping new squadrons in the expansion of Coastal Command. The Shackleton MR.2 was introduced in late 1952, with the prototype having made its first flight on 17 June 1952. Seventy were delivered to the RAF, the first squadron being No. 42 at St Eval.

After nearly five years in RAF service, a new and modernised version was evolved as the Shackleton MR.3. Although very similar to its predecessors, it incorporated a number of new features, not the least of which was the tricycle undercarriage. The twin 20mm guns (aimed by an air gunner seated above the bomb aimer) were retained in the nose, but the mid-upper turret was deleted. The undercarriage was increased to four main landing wheels and twin nosewheels to cope with the projected increase in all-up weight. In order to improve the Shackleton's already impressive range, the MR.3 introduced auxiliary fuel tanks mounted at the wing tips, which increased capacity to 4,248 gallons.

The Shackleton MR.3 made its first flight on 2 September 1955 and thirty-four aircraft were delivered to the RAF. The first to be equipped with the MR.3 was No. 220 Squadron at St Eval. Shortly afterwards, the MR.3 entered service with five more squadrons and the MR.3 became a familiar sight at Coastal Command stations at St Mawgan, Kinloss, Ballykelly, Gibraltar and Malta.

Later, to assist take-offs with heavier loads, the MR.3 Phase 3 aircraft were given two 2,500lb static thrust Bristol-Siddeley Viper 203 auxiliary turbojets mounted in the outer engine nacelles.

In 1957, a trainer version was introduced as the Shackleton T.4. These seventeen aircraft were conversions of older MR.1 aircraft and were used to equip the School of Maritime Reconnaissance at St Mawgan and the Maritime OCU at Kinloss. All armament was deleted but additional radar positions were installed for instructors and pupils. Later, a further ten Shackleton MR.2 aircraft were converted to the T.2 version as training aircraft.

Shackleton Search and Rescue

Twenty-four-hour standbys commenced in 1952, each maritime reconnaissance squadron taking a week in turn. In their heyday, Shackleton aircraft were frequently able to assist stranded mariners by dropping equipment, particularly Lindholme Gear.

Buckets of Sunshine – Nuclear Testing on Christmas Island

The first use of Shackleton aircraft in support of nuclear testing took place when four modified MR.1 aircraft of No. 269 Squadron were detached from RAF Ballykelly to Darwin, Australia, primarily engaged on various weather data-gathering operations over the Timor Sea and Indian Ocean during Operation Mosaic.

A further series of tests were agreed with the Australian Government, under the codename Operation Buffalo. Four Shackleton MR.2 aircraft from No. 204 Squadron were deployed to Pearce AFB in Western Australia. The first British thermonuclear device (Blue Danube) was dropped over the range by Valiant WZ366 on 11 October 1956. With testing completed, the Shackleton aircraft returned to the UK.

The Australian Government declined any further testing on their ranges so a new location on Christmas Island was chosen. Shackleton aircraft from Nos 206 and 240 Squadrons at Ballykelly were chosen to support the operation, although the aircraft had first to be modified at No. 49MU for the work to be undertaken. The first detachment of No. 240 Squadron aircraft flew to Christmas Island at the end of February 1957 and returned to the UK at the end of April, following the successful drop of the first weapon in Operation Grapple 1.

In May 1958, No. 204 Squadron flew to Christmas Island under the codename Operation Grapple Y. They then remained here for the duration of the six H-bomb tests under Grapple Z. In June 1958, they were joined by a detachment from No. 269 Squadron and once the final bomb had been detonated – on 11 September 1958 – all aircraft returned to RAF Ballykelly, arriving home in October.

The Shackleton would eventually remain in service with Coastal Command right up to when it was replaced by the Nimrod MR.1. However, during its long career, it provided excellent service and found itself involved in a number of conflicts. The following are details of some of those conflicts:

The Cyprus Emergency of 1955–56

The worsening political situation in Cyprus during 1955 created a new role for the Shackleton – anti-smuggling patrols to prevent arms reaching the island. No. 38 Squadron, based at RAF Luqa, Malta, were given the task of patrolling the coast of Cyprus and flew their first operation on 21 July 1955. It involved around 250 flying hours of operations per month and eventually lasted for around four years.

When the Governor of Cyprus declared a state of emergency on 27 November 1955, a decision was taken to increase the number of British troops on the island under Exercise Encompass. From December 1955 through to 24 January 1956, this exercise saw numerous trooping flights into the island, many undertaken by Shackleton aircraft from just about every unit operating the type. Trooping flights by Shackleton aircraft then continued on an 'as required' basis up until the emergency ended in December 1959.

Operation Musketeer

When President Nasser of Egypt declared that he intended to nationalise the French- and British-controlled Universal Suez Canal Company, the region was thrown into doubt. The troop-carrying role pioneered by the Shackleton aircraft during the Cyprus Emergency was to play a significant part in getting troops into Egypt under Operation Challenger. The British and French Governments had anticipated President Nasser's actions and already had a plan in place – Operation Musketeer – which they duly activated.

Initially, Shackleton aircraft in the area (from Nos 37 and 38 Squadrons, based at RAF Luqa) were tasked to provide maritime patrols in support of the operation. Later, Shackleton MR.1 aircraft from No. 206 Squadron at St Eval airlifted the 16th Parachute Brigade from Blackbushe to Cyprus.

When a peaceful solution to the problem was found, Shackleton aircraft of Nos 204, 206 and 228 Squadrons brought the troops out of theatre and back to the UK.

Operation Firedog

The Malayan Emergency was a guerrilla war fought between Commonwealth forces and the Malayan National Liberation Army (MNLA), the military arm of the Malayan Communist Party (MCP), from 1948 to 1960. The British and Commonwealth operation became known as Operation Firedog.

In May 1958, No. 205 Squadron from RAF Changi were detached to Seletar and exchanged their Sunderland V aircraft for the new Shackleton MR.1A; these were soon employed on maritime reconnaissance activities, monitoring vessels involved in arms smuggling. These operations continued until the end of the emergency was declared on 31 July 1960.

Jordan

From 1955, the Soviet Union had provided military aid to both Egypt and Syria, including the supply of aircraft and the building of airfields in Syria. These airfields clearly threatened the integrity of both Lebanon and Jordan. In February 1958, the United Arab Republic (UAR) was formed between Egypt and Syria while, simultaneously, Iraq and Jordan agreed to an anti-communist, anti-Nasser Federation. Following the assignation of the Iraqi Prime Minister Nuri al-Said on 15 July, King Hussein of Jordan appealed to Britain the following day for assistance in maintaining stability.

The request was immediately supported and on the next morning 200 troops were moved from Cyprus to Amman by Hastings aircraft. By 18 July, 2,200 troops were in Amman, with reinforcements having been carried on Comet C.2 aircraft supported by ShackletonMR.2 aircraft of Nos 42 and 204 Squadrons, in a troop-carrying role – each carrying thirty-one armed soldiers.

Following an agreement in the region on 11 August 1958, British troops began withdrawing, with the last of them vacating the region on 2 November.

Coastal Command Rotary Wing Activities

The Air Sea Warfare Development Unit (ASWDU) was formed at Thorney Island in May 1948 and was tasked with the development and testing of new maritime equipment. One of its first trials involved the Sikorsky Hoverfly I, which was the very first helicopter used by the RAF. It was the British version of the Sikorsky VS-316, which made its first flight in 1942. It was fitted with either wheels or pontoons and entered service with the Helicopter Training Flight at Andover in May 1945. Forty-five were delivered and were used mainly by No. 529 Squadron.

A small number of Hoverfly I helicopters were trialled with ASWDU during a detachment at Calshot but while the trials were relatively successful, the Hoverfly I did not see regular service with Coastal Command.

The Bristol Sycamore became the first British-designed helicopter to enter service with the RAF at home and overseas. The prototype (VL958) made its first flight on 24 July 1947 and the first production version was developed into the HR.12 search and rescue and anti-submarine reconnaissance version for Coastal Command. The first Sycamore HR.12 (WV781/FZ) was delivered to ASWDU at RAF St Mawgan on 19 February 1952 to begin trials and was joined by a further three airframes (WV782, WV783 and WV784). Following the trials, future variants were developed as the HR.13 and HR.14, the former specialising in the Search and Rescue role. Eventually, the Command had sixteen on strength, dispersed around the UK, when the type provided the RAF's very first bright yellow-painted rescue helicopters.

The Whirlwind helicopter was the Westland-built military version of the Sikorsky S-55 for service with the RAF and Royal Navy. The first Whirlwind HAR.1 for the Royal Navy made its first flight on 15 August 1953, while the Whirlwind HAR.2 began deliveries to the RAF in 1955. Around sixty of this version were produced for both communications and Search and Rescue duties with both Transport and Coastal Commands. The last HAR.2 (XK991) was delivered on 16 November 1957.

The first Coastal Command unit to receive the HAR.2 was No. 22 Squadron, based at Thorney Island, in February 1955. For their rescue operations, the Whirlwind helicopters were painted bright yellow, with both the winch and scoop-net methods being employed for the retrieval of survivors from dinghies.

A detachment of two Search and Rescue helicopters of Coastal Command were permanently based at Leuchars, Acklington, Horsham St Faith, Felixstowe, Thorney Island, Chivenor, Valley, Leconfield and St Mawgan where they provided sterling service.

Farewell to the Sunderland

In January 1957, Coastal Command said farewell to the final Sunderland V squadron. Having come into service with No. 201 Squadron at Pembroke Dock in early 1945, their services were dispensed with at the end of February 1957, marking the end of a very long and successful association between the Sunderland and Coastal Command.

Meteorological Research

After the Second World War, meteorological research remained the domain of Coastal Command. Initial equipment was the Halifax GR.6 variant, which remained in service with No. 202 Squadron at RAF Aldergrove from October 1946 to May 1951, when it was replaced by the Handley Page Hastings. The No. 202 Squadron aircraft were fitted with the Dobson-Brewer frost point hygrometer that had also become a fundamental instrument of the Meteorological Research Flight (MRF), and accurate low-level flying was facilitated by early radio altimeters. A small number of GR.VI aircraft were converted into the Met.6 variant and used by the MRF at Farnborough for research into cloud structure and atmospheric characteristics at medium and low level.

In October 1950, the delivery of Hastings Met.1 aircraft began with No. 202 Squadron at Aldergrove, eventually replacing the Halifax Met.6 in service by May 1951. The Hastings Met.1 was a specially converted aircraft designed for use by Coastal Command on metrological research activities. With the predominant weather in the UK arriving from the west, much of this Met research activity was conducted over the Atlantic Ocean. The information was radioed back to base and then flashed to the Central Forecasting Office at Dunstable, which helped form the basis of daily weather reports.

Coastal Command's No. 202 Squadron was based at RAF Aldergrove and continued to operate the Hastings until disbanded on 28 August 1964. After being withdrawn from service with No. 202 Squadron, the Hastings Met.1 aircraft was then returned to C.1 standard and re-entered service with Transport Command.

Post-war, the Lancaster formed an important part of Coastal Command operations. This image, taken in early 1946, depicts a No. 279 Squadron Lancaster ASR.3, serial number RF310/RL-A, complete with under-fuselage life raft. No. 279 Squadron was resident at RAF Beccles, with a detachment at Pegu, but was disbanded on 10 March 1946. After being damaged in an incident, RF310 was struck off charge on 11 April 1946. (*Crown Copyright/Air Historical Branch image PRB-1-739*)

No. 203 Squadron equipped with the Lancaster GR.3 in July 1946 and retained the aircraft until March 1953. This image shows Lancaster GR.3 SW377 although the date of the image is unknown. (*Crown Copyright/Air Historical Branch image AHB-Lanc-GR3-203Sqn*)

'Q' DINGHY UNDER TOW AT 8-10 KNOTS IN SEA.
(SCALE I)

A.S.W.D.U. G439   HELICOPTER TRIAL.   PLATE .4.

An interesting view of an early Sikorsky Hoverfly I helicopter in service with the newly formed Air-Sea Warfare Development Unit (ASWDU) at RAF Thorney Island; it is seen during early trials at a detachment at Calshot and was photographed with a dingy in tow. The Hoverfly I was the first helicopter to be used by the RAF. It was first flown in 1942 and fitted with either wheels or pontoons and entered service at the Helicopter Training Flight at Andover on 9 May 1945. However, the Flight was disbanded on 16 January 1946. (*Crown Copyright/Air Historical Branch image CHP-1*)

Sunderland V VB389/NS-D of No. 201 Squadron after landing at Havel Lake, with its contents being loaded onto barges, during Operation Plainfare in September 1948. The tonnage carried by the flying boats was relatively small, but the Berliners were impressed with their contribution. Sunderland aircraft continued to operate until December 1948, by which time the airlift by land-based aircraft into Berlin's airfields had increased considerably. (*Crown Copyright/Air Historical Branch image R-1831*)

Sunderland V SZ568/TA-C of No. 235 OCU at Calshot during 1950. SZ568 remained with No. 235 OCU when it was re-designated as the Flying Boat Training Squadron at Pembroke Dock in October 1953 and the aircraft then served until October 1956, when it was struck off charge. (*Crown Copyright/ Air Historical Branch image PRB-1-858*)

The prototype Shackleton MR.1, VW126, pictured in 1950 while the aircraft was undergoing trials with the A&AEE. This image shows the 20mm cannons that were fitted on each side on the nose of the aircraft, which were removed from later production aircraft. (*Crown Copyright/Air Historical Branch image PRB-1-894*)

A Halifax Met.6 meteorological research aircraft, serial number ST796, in flight on 16 June 1950. The aircraft was one of two Halifax Met.6 aircraft used by the Meteorological Research Flight (MRF) at Farnborough and with No. 202 Squadron at RAF Aldergrove between 1946 and 1950 for research into cloud structure and atmospheric characteristics at medium and low level. A typical Halifax crew of seven would comprise two pilots, two met observers, a navigator, a flight engineer and a signaller. The No. 202 Squadron aircraft were fitted with the Dobson-Brewer frost point hygrometer that had also become a fundamental instrument of the MRF, with accurate low-level flying being facilitated by early radio altimeters. (*Crown Copyright/Air Historical Branch image PRB-1-431*)

Above: Initial deliveries of Shackleton MR.1 aircraft were made to No. 120 Squadron at RAF Kinloss in March 1951, then to the ASWDU at St Mawgan. This aircraft is thought to be VP284/B and was photographed while operating with No. 236 OCU at RAF Kinloss. (*Crown Copyright/Air Historical Branch image PRB-1-9531*)

Right: An early Shackleton MR.1 (unidentified, but coded B-V) of the Joint Anti-Submarine School (JASS) at RAF Ballykelly in January 1952. The JASS ran courses to teach tactical doctrine and conduct anti-submarine warfare (ASW) with an emphasis on the development and application of combined tactics. JASS operated three Shackleton MR.1 aircraft and usually provided the 'opposition' air component, carrying out shadowing of the surface forces on behalf of the submarines during exercises mounted jointly by the Royal Navy and RAF for personnel on the courses. This image appears to have been 'retouched', thereby improving the contrast between the sea and the aircraft. (*Crown Copyright/Air Historical Branch image X-42493*)

After Coastal Command's B-17 Fortress and B-24 Liberator aircraft had been returned to the US at the conclusion of the Lend-Lease arrangement, the Lancaster GR.3 became the RAF's principal land-based maritime reconnaissance aircraft until the arrival of the former US Navy Neptune aircraft, which were to be supplied under the MDAP programme. This Lancaster GR.3 of No. 210 Squadron was photographed at RAF St Mawgan on 24 May 1952. (*Crown Copyright/Air Historical Branch image PRB-1-4641*)

Bristol Sycamore HR.12 WV781/FZ, of the Air Sea Warfare Development Unit (ASWDU) for trials with Coastal Command, was also photographed at RAF St Mawgan on 24 May 1952. The helicopter had been delivered to the unit on 19 February and was the first British-designed helicopter to enter service with the RAF, at home or overseas. (*Crown Copyright/Air Historical Branch image PRB-1-4639*)

The first Lockheed Neptune MR.1 supplied to the RAF under the Mutual Defence Aid Program, WX493, was photographed at RAF St Eval on 13 January 1952. Fifty-two former US Navy aircraft were operated by Coastal Command as a stop-gap measure until 1957, when they were replaced by the Avro Shackleton. (*Crown Copyright/Air Historical Branch image PRB-1-4153*)

Shortly after entering service with Coastal Command, Shackleton MR.1 aircraft were soon involved in a number of NATO detachments, as well as exercises and goodwill tours. The aircraft was well-suited to this kind of work as it was able carry its own ground crew and a good supply of spares in the large fuselage as well as within luggage panniers located in the bomb bay. The first tour was undertaken by Shackleton MR.1A aircraft of No. 220 Squadron, who visited Ceylon between February and April 1952. (*Crown Copyright/Air Historical Branch image CMP-559*)

The Saunders-Roe (Saro) airborne lifeboat was tested aboard the prototype Shackleton. However, the arrangement was discarded at an early stage in favour of the more efficient Lindholme Gear. This image shows lifeboat number 801 fitted to an early Shackleton MR.1. (*Crown Copyright/Air Historical Branch image PRB-1-10733*)

The first 'full prototype' of the Shackleton MR.2 – WB833 – was photographed in flight during October 1952. The MR.2 had a redesigned and lengthened nose and a new elongated tail with an observation post to aid visual searches. (*Crown Copyright/Air Historical Branch image PRB-1-5544a*)

Following No. 220 Squadron's deployment to Ceylon in 1952, No. 42 Squadron were deployed to Ceylon in 1953 with their newer MR.2 aircraft. While on the trip they also sent a small detachment on to South Africa. Shackleton MR.2s of No. 42 Squadron – including WG554/A-A and WG556/A-J – were photographed while flying over Durban on 22 April 1953. The tour to the Far East and South Africa in April and May 1953 covered a total of 17,740 miles. (*Crown Copyright/Air Historical Branch image CFP-744*)

The first Lockheed Neptune MR.1 was delivered to the RAF's Coastal Command on 27 January 1952. It entered service with No. 217 Squadron, initially at St Eval and later at RAF Kinloss. The No. 217 Squadron crew of WX505/A-J were photographed at the end of a sortie at RAF Kinloss on 28 May 1953. (*Crown Copyright/Air Historical Branch image PRB-1-6487*)

During a training flight from RAF Kinloss on 28 May 1953, Neptune MR.1 WX505/A-J, of No. 217 Squadron, demonstrated its single-engine performance, having shut down and feathered its starboard engine. (*Crown Copyright/Air Historical Branch image PRB-1-6503*)

Shackleton MR.2 WL796 made its first flight on 23 August 1953 and was exhibited at the SBAC Show at Farnborough the following month, equipped with an airborne lifeboat for air-sea rescue duties. However, the aircraft never deployed it operationally. (*Crown Copyright/Air Historical Branch image AHB-MIS-AVRO-480-017*)

Short Sunderland V RN290/B-Z, of No.230 Squadron, moored at Tower Bridge during Battle of Britain Day celebrations on 17 September 1953. It was photographed in the company of Air-Sea Rescue launch No. 2594 of the RAF Marine Branch. (*Crown Copyright/Air Historical Branch image X-47317-2*)

Shackleton MR.1A VP293/A-F of No. 42 Squadron (nearest the camera), in company with an unidentified MR.2 variant (coded B-Z and thought to be WL742) of No. 206 Squadron, was photographed flying over a Royal Navy vessel on 14 May 1954. (*Crown Copyright/Air Historical Branch image X-50909*)

Meteorological research activities post-war continued with Coastal Command. This image depicts a Hastings Met.1 aircraft (TG616) over the Atlantic on a weather reconnaissance sortie on 9 August 1954. The information was radioed back to base and then flashed to the Central Forecasting Office at Dunstable, helping to form the basis of daily weather reports. Coastal Command's No. 202 Squadron was based at RAF Aldergrove and continued to operate the Hastings until disbanded on 31 July 1964. (*Crown Copyright/Air Historical Branch image PRB-1-8568a*)

Sunderland V aircraft of No. 201 Squadron, based at Pembroke Dock, in flight on 3 May 1956. Having received the type in early 1945, the squadron continued to fly the venerable aircraft until it was disbanded at the end of February 1957. The aircraft nearest the camera (SZ576/A-A) was sold to the French navy in July 1957. (*Crown Copyright/Air Historical Branch image PRB-1-11601*)

Taken at Blackbushe on 12 January 1956, this image depicts the first of twenty-eight Coastal Command Shackleton aircraft, drawn from eight squadrons, commencing the airlift of troops from the Parachute Regiment to Cyprus, in order to counter the threat of an uprising by Cypriot Nationalists (EOKA). (*Crown Copyright/Air Historical Branch image PRB-1-11071*)

The Whirlwind helicopter was the Westland-built military version of the Sikorsky S-55, for service with the RAF and the Royal Navy. The first variant for the RAF was the HAR.2, with deliveries commencing in 1955, including those to No. 22 Squadron, RAF Coastal Command, on search and rescue (SAR) duties. This image, taken on 11 July 1956, shows a No. 22 Squadron Whirlwind HAR.2, XJ729, during a mountain rescue training flight from its base at RAF Valley. (*Crown Copyright/Air Historical Branch image T-350*)

Shackleton MR.2 WL737/D of No. 42 Squadron, photographed at Sharjah in July 1957. The Shackleton aircraft carried fragmentation bombs and were involved with RAF operations against the Omani Liberation Army (OLA) during the crisis in Oman. (*Crown Copyright/ Air Historical Branch image CMP-909*)

This Shackleton MR.2 (thought to be WR952/E) of No. 42 Squadron was photographed while conducting operations against rebel tribesmen near Aden in 1957. No. 42 Squadron were normally based at RAF St Eval but had deployed four Shackleton aircraft on rotation to Khormaksar, Aden, in January 1957. (*Crown Copyright/Air Historical Branch image CMP-935*)

An RTTL (Rescue/ Target-Towing Launch) II of No. 1107 Marine Craft Unit, part of the RAF Air/Sea Rescue Service, photographed while at speed off Newhaven around the south coast of England in September 1958. This particular vessel, HMAFV 2758, was built by Vosper Ltd, Portsmouth, in 1957 as an RTTL. It was later converted to a Fast Motor Yacht and subsequently to a luxury vessel based in Malta. (*Crown Copyright/ Air Historical Branch image T-656*)

The Final Years (1960–69)

No. 203 Squadron re-equipped with Shackleton MR.3 aircraft in June 1966 and in February 1969 were detached to RAF Luqa, Malta, where, shortly afterwards, XF708/C was photographed near to Valletta Harbour. XF708/C is preserved in its former No. 203 Squadron colours at the Imperial War Museum at Duxford. (*Crown Copyright/Air Historical Branch image TN-1-3831*)

For Coastal Command, the 1960s continued much as the 1950s had ended. The Shackleton was still the primary maritime reconnaissance platform, and would remain so right up to the end of the Command itself. Search and Rescue helicopter duties were still being handled by the Whirlwind HAR.2 although its replacement, the HAR.10, was on the horizon. Meteorological research was still being conducted by Hasting Met.1 aircraft with No. 202 Squadron at Aldergrove, but that was scheduled to change. The thorny issue of a suitable replacement for the venerable Shackleton was still being 'discussed' in the corridors of power. Financial constraints continued to place pressure on reducing the strength of the Command. Sadly, the 1960s were to be the last decade of operations for Coastal Command.

Shackleton Operations and Deployments

The Coastal Command Shackleton fleet – seemingly diminishing at every strategic or cost-cutting review – continued to soldier on. The number of conflicts with which Coastal Command and the Shackleton fleet were involved during the decade continued to rise and the following are a small selection of their activities:

In 1961, around 40 per cent of the UK's oil came from Kuwait. It was no surprise, then, that when General Abdul Qarim Kassem declared on 25 June that Kuwait was now part of Iraq, the

British Government acted sharply. On 30 June the Emir of Kuwait appealed for help, and the British Cabinet approved significant military action for the Royal Navy and RAF, with limited participation for Coastal Command. A pair of Shackleton aircraft from No. 37 Squadron moved up to Bahrain from Khormaksar to provide reconnaissance capabilities in the area. The crisis ended peacefully and Britain's oil supplies were protected.

In 1962, a General Strike was called in British Guiana, threatening the stability of the country. British Army units were sent to Georgetown from Jamaica and the UK. In addition, a detachment of Shackleton MR.2 aircraft was sent from Jamaica in a show of force. In 1966, the colony became independent as Guyana, under a coalition government, and most British servicemen left soon afterwards.

It was the ambition of Indonesia's President Soekarno to unite Malaya, the Philippines and Indonesia within an Indonesian empire. Once again, assistance was requested from the British Government, which was duly approved. Initially, three Shackleton MR.2 aircraft (WG555, WR964 and WR966) of No. 204 Squadron were sent from Ballykelly to Changi in May 1964 to provide patrols to determine what Indonesian land forces were doing. They only stayed for twelve days. However, the 'Confrontation' situation worsened and further Shackleton activity took place. Once again, Ballykelly provided the support, with aircraft of No. 203 Squadron being moved to Changi to support No. 205 Squadron already resident. Once again, reconnaissance was provided over the Strait of Malacca under the codename Operation Hawk Moth. No. 203 Squadron returned to Ballykelly in October 1965, leaving No. 205 Squadron at Changi. There was an attempted coup in Djakarta; the military counter-coup essentially ended Soekarno's rule and the prospect of peace seemed likely. Peace talks continued and the British forces were withdrawn from the region in August of the following year.

On 11 November 1965, Ian Smith made a unilateral declaration of Independence (UDI) from Britain on behalf of Southern Rhodesia. The British response was to impose sanctions on imports and exports; a military solution (white-on-white) was considered untenable. Early in 1966, the first detachment of three Shackleton MR.2 aircraft of No. 37 Squadron were sent to Majunga airfield on French-controlled Malagasy. They were tasked with providing air reconnaissance of the area, especially suspicious shipping, the details of which were relayed to the Royal Navy, who would investigate. These joint Coastal Command-Royal Navy patrols were named 'Beira Patrols'. No. 37 Squadron were replaced by No. 38 Squadron later in the year, and in February 1967 it was the turn of No. 42 Squadron. This arrangement continued until February 1972, when it became the responsibility of Nos 204 and 210 Squadrons. The 'Beira Patrols' were progressively reduced in size until they finally ceased in 1978. Following political infighting within Southern Rhodesia, Ian Smith finally agreed to the Internal Settlement with non-militant nationalists in 1978. Under these terms the country was reconstituted under black rule as Zimbawe Rhodesia in 1979 but this new order was rejected by the guerrillas and the international community. Following further political activities, Ian Smith revoked UDA as part of the Lancaster House Agreement signed in June 1979 and following further direct British rule, the UK granted independence to Zimbabwe in 1980.

Soviet Trawlers et al

During the early 1960s, the Soviet Navy and the Communist Bloc's fishing fleet began operating around the British Isles in increasing numbers. Once it had been highlighted by fisherman complaining of their presence, and then by various media reports, the British public took an interest. Operation Chacewater was launched, in which Coastal Command began monitoring their movements, in particular those 'trawlers' and other vessels which loitered in areas covering the arrival and departure routes for the Royal Navy submarine fleet. Shortly afterwards, counter operations such as Operation Adjutant were conducted, seeking out Soviet submarines operating in the area.

The main threat from the Soviet Northern Fleet was in the Atlantic and, by 1965, most of Coastal Command's activities were concentrated within No. 18 Group, based in Scotland, to monitor their activities. No recorded confrontation with Soviet submarines was recorded around this time although both the Shackleton aircraft from RAF Ballykelly and frigates operating out of Londonderry would make contact with Soviet submarines while carrying out surveillance off the mouth of Lough Foyle.

The Cuban Missile Crisis

The Cuban Missile Crisis erupted in October 1962 when US President John F. Kennedy called the Russians' bluff and threatened military action if the Soviet Union did not remove the missile installations on Cuba.

The CIA had been aware of a significant increase in Soviet vessels berthing in Cuban ports, thought to be around thirty-eight in just seven weeks, and then related this information to an instinct that the Soviet Union would base Inter-continental Range Ballistic Missiles (IRBM) on Cuba. Immediately, Agency (CIA) U-2 flights over Cuba were increased and on 29 August 1962, an Agency U-2 returned with images of two S-75 Dvina surface-to-air missile (SAM) sites on the island, along with another six more sites under construction. It was soon realised that the layout of the SAM sites was very similar to the specific layout used when protecting ballistic missile bases in the Soviet Union. U-2 flights over Cuba continued, and by 16 October the US had photographic evidence of an SS-4 Sandal MRBM site in an advanced state of construction. Meanwhile, RAF Valiant B(PR).1 aircraft from No. 543 Squadron (which had conveniently been located in Jamaica, flying survey missions in the wake of Hurricane Hattie) had conducted a number of photographic reconnaissance flights over Cuba on behalf of the CIA. In addition, photographs of Soviet aircraft being reassembled on the island after shipping from the Soviet Union were plentiful. The Cuban Missile Crisis had begun.

On 20 October, Coastal Command operational squadrons began increased patrols over Soviet shipping around the UK and on 23 October the entire operational Shackleton force was placed at six-hour readiness.

Meanwhile a strategic force was being readied, primarily consisting of SAC B-52 and B-47 aircraft, while a pair of Atlas missiles was test-launched from Vandenberg AFB in California. The RAF contributed to the strategic plan with all 144 of its V-bomber force brought to ten-minute readiness. Finally, a large US Navy invasion force was prepared.

At 10:00 hours on 28 October the crisis ended when the Soviet Union agreed to dismantle the missiles, under inspection. President Khrushchev accepted the American terms for the removal of offensive weapons in exchange for guarantees that the US would not invade Cuba.

Whirlwind HAR.10

When the Whirlwind HAR.10 entered service with the RAF, it was the first aircraft powered by a turbine engine. The prototype of the Gnome-powered Whirlwind HAR.10 made its first flight on 28 February 1959 and could be distinguished from earlier piston-engine Whirlwind helicopters by the lengthened fuselage nose.

Production for the RAF totalled sixty-seven and these were delivered from 1961 to 1964. Initial deliveries were made to No. 225 Squadron, Transport Command, with later deliveries going to Flying Training Command and eventually Coastal Command, where it served with Nos 22 (from August 1962), 202 (from August 1964) and 228 Squadrons (from September 1962). At No. 22 Squadron, the new all-yellow Whirlwind rescue helicopters replaced the earlier HAR.2 version and operated at all of the previous detachment locations.

Nimrod MR.1

Evolved from the well-tried Comet transport aircraft, the Nimrod MR.1 was chosen as the replacement for the ageing fleet of Shackleton maritime reconnaissance aircraft. Two prototype Nimrod aircraft (XV148 and XV147) were produced, both converted from civil Comet aircraft. The first prototype was built at Chester and powered by four Rolls-Royce Spey engines (later the chosen powerplant for the type), making its first flight on 23 May 1967. The second prototype was built at Woodford and powered by four Rolls-Royce Avon engines, making its first flight on 31 July 1967.

The first production aircraft (XV226) made its maiden flight on 28 June 1968 and was the first land-based, four-jet maritime reconnaissance aircraft to enter service in any of the world's air forces. The Nimrod MR.1 reflected the very latest concepts in anti-submarine warfare. It provided an on-station patrol time of more than six hours at a range of up to 1,150 miles from base.

The first of forty-five Nimrod MR.1 aircraft (XV230) was handed over to the RAF on 1 October 1969 and was initially delivered to the Nimrod OCU at Kinloss. Coastal Command had been asking for a suitable Shackleton replacement for many years. Sadly, it arrived in time for less than eight weeks' service in their command!

Reorganisation Sees the End of Coastal Command

During 1969, a review of the Royal Air Force was undertaken, recognising its shrinking nature. As a consequence of the review, the decision was taken to absorb Coastal Command as No. 18 (Maritime) Group of Strike Command – bringing to an end a thirty-three-year tradition as guardian of the skies over the seas that surround Britain, as well as the sea lanes that throughout history have been her lifeline to the rest of the world.

As Air Marshal Sir John Lapsley took the salute at the disbandment parade on 27 November 1969, two SAR Whirlwind helicopters, nine Shackleton aircraft and a single Nimrod MR.1 overflew St Mawgan, signalling that Coastal Command was no more.

Throughout their existence, they had conducted a variety of tasks, often under-equipped and during both good and bad times. It had truly lived up to the motto on its coat of arms – Constant Endeavour.

A Shackleton MR.3 thought to be from No. 201 Squadron, photographed at RAF St Mawgan in April 1960. It demonstrated the ten-man flight crew and the corresponding ground crew, all along with weapons available for use and the ground equipment required to operate the aircraft. (*Crown Copyright/ Air Historical Branch image T-1859*)

Above: Shackleton MR.3 XF707/P, of No. 201 Squadron, based at RAF St Mawgan, was photographed during a low-level maritime patrol sortie in November 1960. (*Crown Copyright/Air Historical Branch image PRB-1-20153*)

Right: Shackleton WG556/A of No. 224 Squadron, photographed in 1960 while operating a maritime patrol sortie from its Gibraltar base while in support of a Royal Navy vessel. No. 224 Squadron was disbanded on 31 October 1966, while WG556 ended its life with the BDRF and, later, the fire section at RAF Lossiemouth before being scrapped in July 1982. (*Crown Copyright/ Air Historical Branch image CMP-1301*)

When it became clear that the RAF could not preserve a Sunderland – with the lack of staging facilities combined with the significant costs of flying one back to the UK – it emerged that the Aéronavale (French navy) operated three Sunderland aircraft from Toulon. They were approached and agreed to donate one of their aircraft to the RAF Museum. Sunderland V ML824 made its final flight from Lanveoc-Pouloc, near Brest, to Pembroke Dock on 24 March 1961. En route, she rendezvoused with a pair of No. 201 Squadron Shackleton aircraft (from her old squadron) over the Bishop Rock and then flew in formation via St David's and Pembroke. The two St Mawgan-based Shackleton MR.3 aircraft were WR975/O and WR980/P. ML824 is now preserved in the RAF Museum at Hendon. (*Crown Copyright/Air Historical Branch image PRB-1-20681*)

An image taken during NATO Exercise Dawn Breeze in March 1962, off the Iberian Peninsula. This Shackleton MR.3 (unidentified but coded 'F' of No. 206 Squadron) was photographed during a simulated attack on a Royal Navy submarine. Note that the Shackleton has its bomb bay doors open for the attack. (*Crown Copyright/Air Historical Branch image PRB-1-22420*)

This image shows armourers from No. 224 Squadron loading a rack of six depth charges into the bomb bay of a Shackleton MR.2, WG533/B, at RAF Gibraltar in March 1962 during NATO Exercise Dawn Breeze. (*Crown Copyright/Air Historical Branch PRB-22437*)

Once the depth charges have been loaded into the bomb bay, a pair of light series carriers (seen here in white) are added and positioned on either side of the depth charges. (*Crown Copyright/Air Historical Branch PRB-22436*)

Armourers at RAF Kinloss were photographed while preparing to load an active sonobuoy onto a No. 120 Squadron Shackleton MR.2 ahead of NATO Exercise Fairwind Seven in June 1962. To the right of the trolley (numbered 13, 9 and 4) are passive sonobuoys while to the left of the trolley are the active sonobuoys. (*Crown Copyright/Air Historical Branch PRB-23207*)

An RAF Marine Branch Pinnace high-speed launch, number 1381, proceeding across Plymouth Sound off Fort Picklecombe from its base at Mount Batten to the squadron training area for maritime weapons recovery duties on 26 September 1963. (*Crown Copyright/Air Historical Branch image T-4272*)

Shackleton MR.2C WL738/D of No. 37 Squadron, flying over the Federation of Southern Arabia (now Yemen) during operations in the Radfan region of the country in 1964. At the time of the photograph, the squadron was based at RAF Khormaksar, Aden. (*Crown Copyright/Air Historical Branch image T-4646*)

An unidentified Shackleton MR.3 aircraft, coded 'C' (although thought to be XF708) of No. 203 Squadron, from RAF Luqa, Malta, was photographed over the MV *Mary Lou* and its tug in the Mediterranean shortly after the squadron took up residence on the island in February 1969. Shackleton aircraft remained on the island until the type was eventually replaced with the new Nimrod MR.1 in October 1971. (*Crown Copyright/Air Historical Branch image TN-1-2618*)

The aircraft Coastal Command needed so badly, but only enjoyed the benefits of for a matter of weeks! The second prototype Nimrod MR.1, serial number XV148, photographed at the Hawker Siddeley (later BAe) facility at Woodford ahead of a test flight. The aircraft was converted from a civil Comet airliner and was powered by Rolls-Royce Avon engines. XV148 made its first flight at Woodford on 31 July 1967. (*Crown Copyright/Air Historical Branch image T-7784a*)

The first of forty-six Nimrod MR.1 aircraft was handed over to the RAF on 1 October 1969 and was soon operating with No. 236 OCU before entering squadron service with five squadrons. Less than eight weeks later, on 27 October 1969, RAF Coastal Command was no longer, having been absorbed into RAF Strike Command. This photograph shows Nimrod MR.1 XV254, of No. 42 Squadron at RAF St Mawgan, working with a pair of Royal Navy submarines on 10 August 1971. (*Crown Copyright/Air Historical Branch image TN-1-6451-21*)

Bibliography and Sources

Andrews, C.F. and E.B. Morgan, *Vickers Aircraft since 1908*, Putnam, 2nd edition, 1988.

Andrews, C.F. and E.B. Morgan, *Supermarine Aircraft since 1914*, Putnam, 3rd edition, 1989.

Ashworth, Chris, *RAF Coastal Command 1936–1969*, Patrick Stephens Ltd, 1992.

Barnes, C.H., *Handley Page Aircraft since 1907*, Putnam, 2nd edition, 1987.

British Aviation Research Group, *British Military Aircraft Serials and Markings*, British Aviation Research Group, 2nd edition, 1983.

Carter, Ian, *Coastal Command 1939–1945*, Ian Allan Ltd, 2004.

Conyers-Nesbit, Roy, *The Strike Wings – Special Anti-Shipping Squadrons 1942–1945*, William Kimber & Co. Ltd, 1984.

Conyers-Nesbit, Roy, *Coastal Command in Action 1939–1945*, Sutton Publishing, 1997.

Flintham, Victor, *Air Wars and Aircraft – A Detailed Record of Air Combat, 1945 to the Present*, Arms and Armour Press, 1989.

Franks, Norman, *Coastal Command's Air War Against the German U-boat*, Pen & Sword Aviation, 2014.

James, Derek N., *Westland Aircraft since 1915*, Putnam, 2nd edition, 1995.

Jefford, C.G., *RAF Squadrons*, Airlife Publishing Ltd, 2nd edition, 2001.

McNeill, Ross, *Royal Air Force Coastal Command Losses of the Second World War – Volume 1*, Midland Publishing, 2003.

Robertson, Bruce, *British Military Aircraft Serials 1878–1987*, Midland Counties Publications, 6th edition, 1987.

Sturtivant, Ray, *Flying Training and Support Units since 1912*, Air Britain (Historians) Ltd, 2007.

Thetford, Owen, *Aircraft of the Royal Air Force since 1918*, Putnam, 8th edition, 1988.

Wilson, Keith, *Avro Shackleton Owner's Workshop Manual*, Haynes Publishing, 2015.

Wilson, Keith, *RAF in Camera: 1950s*, Pen & Sword Aviation, 2015.

Wilson, Keith, *RAF in Camera: 1960s*, Pen & Sword Aviation, 2015.

Wilson, Keith, *RAF in Camera: 1970s*, Pen & Sword Aviation, 2017.

Coastal Command – The Air Ministry Account of the Part Played by Coastal Command in the Battle of the Sea 1939–1942, HMSO, 1943.

Plus the following papers and magazines:

Various issues of *The Aeroplane*, *Flight* and *Flight International* magazines.